The Anxiety Handbook

The Anxiety Handbook

THE 7-STEP PLAN

to Understand, Manage and Overcome Anxiety

CALISTOGA PRESS

Contents

Introduction

There appears to be much to worry about these days. Economic upheaval has grown such that many people struggle with two or even three jobs just to make ends meet. Disturbances in world peace make something as simple as air travel seem complex and intimidating. Social networking sites, instant messaging, and texting have all but replaced simple phone calls, let alone direct face-to-face communication. Daily life seems to grow even more complicated every day.

Perhaps it shouldn't come as a surprise that nearly two in every ten Americans—or around fifty million people in the United States—suffer from anxiety disorders each year. Indeed, anxiety is the number one mental health condition affecting women today, and the number two mental health condition affecting men—second only to alcohol and drug abuse.

With so many self-help gurus making it seem so easy to live a happy and fulfilled life, you might feel you're abnormal because you worry all the time. Worrying is part and parcel of today's stresses, so you shouldn't feel as if there's something wrong with you if you're one of the millions who suffer from anxiety. When it comes to worrying, a big question is, do you control your worries, or do you let your worries control you?

Whether you bought this book because you're having trouble managing your own anxious feelings, or you have a loved one who is suffering from debilitating anxiety, have confidence that you can get the anxiety under control. Anxiety is a feeling—no different from happiness or sadness—which means that it can be managed and (strange as this may sound) even be made to be helpful. Even if you've already been diagnosed with an anxiety disorder, know that anxiety is a treatable mental health condition. Although anxiety may feel mysterious and all-consuming at times, there is a science to it. Understanding what anxiety is and familiarizing yourself with the known ways to manage anxiety can help you achieve immediate relief and long-term change. Beginning this book is a good first step in the right direction.

Congratulate yourself for taking positive action—this in itself is a great step toward curbing anxiety! Now let's get started.

HOW THIS BOOK IS ORGANIZED

This book revolves around seven steps you can take to minimize your experience of anxiety. The steps are divided into three sections, with each section providing information on a unique aspect of anxiety and how to deal with it.

The first section, "Understanding Anxiety," provides an overview of anxiety—its nature, symptoms, causes, and types. Understanding what anxiety (or any such condition) is and where it comes from are the first steps toward managing and ultimately overcoming it. The mystery and surprise that seem to surround anxiety are at least part of the reason why anxiety itself can feel so overwhelming. Breaking the malady down into its components can make it less intimidating.

The second section, "Managing Anxiety," presents easy-to-follow steps on dealing with anxiety whenever it appears. The tips provided are known to be effective and can provide immediate relief, as well as get you more in tune with your own feelings, emotions, and possible triggers. Among the tips that will be discussed are thought management, emotional intelligence, and behavioral techniques.

Last, the third section discusses "Overcoming Anxiety." While it is important to understand what anxiety is and where it comes from, and it is helpful to be able to suppress an episode when it occurs, truly overcoming anxiety ultimately has to do with long-term lifestyle changes. This section will look at the ways in which things like diet and exercise can impact overall mental health, talk about the potential benefits of certain medications, and strategize ways to cope with anxiety-inducing people and situations.

HOW TO USE THIS BOOK

Although this book is presented as a seven-step guide to understanding, managing, and ultimately overcoming the symptoms of anxiety, it's not necessary to follow the steps in exactly the order they are presented. You may choose to read it through from cover to cover, or you may find that certain steps apply to your situation more directly. Not everyone responds the same way to the same techniques, and each reader's anxiety is different. As you gain understanding and insight into your own issues, you can begin forming a plan to rid yourself of unnecessary anxiety, whether you march through the seven steps in order or use only some of them. You may find that some approaches work better than others; if so, use them—there are no "wrong answers" here. Use what works.

Additionally, readers may benefit from working with an "accountability partner"—someone who will hold you accountable for reading and using the exercises in this book. Like a gym buddy or a dieting partner, this person can help provide encouragement and, when necessary, give a friendly nudge to get you back on track when you find yourself slacking off. You don't have to fight anxiety alone, and having an accountability partner is a good way to get over whatever fears might stand in the way of conquering your anxiety issues.

A disclaimer: Please note that reading this book does not replace a consultation with a licensed physician or mental health professional. It's always best to consult with your health care providers to tailor a treatment plan to your individual needs. The publisher is also not responsible for any consequences that result from following medical and psychotherapeutic procedures discussed in this book.

Understanding Anxiety

STEP **1**

Understand the Types and Characteristics of Anxiety

STEP **2**

*Understand the Roots and Causes of Anxiety
and Related Conditions*

....

The first section of this book takes a close look at what exactly
anxiety is and where it comes from. It's a lot easier to solve a
problem when you really know what that problem is. With this
in mind, let's take a look at common types of anxiety disorders as
well as common causes of symptoms.

Understand the Types and Characteristics of Anxiety

If you're reading this book, chances are you've already come face-to-face with anxiety in one way or another. Maybe you have experienced anxiety yourself, or have seen symptoms in someone you care about. Since anxiety impacts different people in different ways, it can be difficult to describe clinically; it's unpleasant, nerve-racking, frustrating, jittery—a collection of just about every negative emotion you can imagine. The onset is often quick, and the impact can be pervasive—anxiety can interfere with every aspect of daily life. Even when your rational mind tries to take over, telling you there's nothing to be afraid of or that you "shouldn't" feel this way, the anxiety often remains, steadfastly refusing to listen to reason. Getting rid of this emotional reaction is easier said than done. Consider the following examples.

PERFORMANCE ANXIETY

Your boss just handed you a once-in-a-lifetime opportunity. For a limited time, you will be in charge of a high-risk, high-reward project for the company, and your performance will determine whether or not you're up for promotion. The pressure is high, and it could be a big turning point in your career. Perform well, and you will be on the fast track to the peak of your career; perform poorly, and you may be considered incapable of rising any further.

What begins as a new and exciting prospect can often turn quickly into anxiety. Thoughts of potential success may be obscured by recurring thoughts of the possibility of failure, to the point where worry can take up a lot of the time that could have been spent developing your new career. You may experience physical symptoms, and the very idea of your presentation to your boss might make you feel tense, irritable, and nauseated. The words "what if" become their own terrible block between you and the rest of your life. Of course, being anxious about trying something new or being put in the spotlight is perfectly normal, but when that anxiety progresses to the point where it is debilitating and affects your performance, it really becomes a problem.

FEAR BY ASSOCIATION

Something about buttons—large buttons on clothing—sets you on edge. Just the sight of oversized fasteners on clothes, bags, anything at all, and you become ridiculously agitated. The larger the button, the worse you feel. It's so bad that you've demanded that your family never buy or wear clothing with buttons on them!

Rationally, you know that this is a ridiculous fear; a button is a simple, useful, largely harmless object. However, somewhere in your past, perhaps something happened to you that made you associate buttons with being terrified. Perhaps someone wearing a coat with large buttons tried to hurt you when you were a child; it could have also been something as simple as accidentally choking on a button that you had stuck into your mouth when you were still an infant. The event could have been innocent in truth but terrifying to you at a young age, with lasting effects.

A classic example is the adult afraid of clowns; perhaps a clown unintentionally terrified you with a sudden action or a popping balloon when you were small and insecure. Whatever the event, the lasting effect is a fear based in your own reality and history.

A BRUSH WITH DISASTER

When a powerful hurricane devastated your area, you bore witness to destruction and turmoil that few experience. Wind took away the roof of the house next door as if it were merely paper; the roaring sound penetrated even the interior bathroom where you lay in the tub, covered with thick padding to protect yourself. You worried about your family in the next county, about your neighbors and friends, and about your own survival.

Since that day, the dark clouds announcing a simple rainstorm fill you with dread. A puddle of water outside your door makes you begin to tremble, and a clap of thunder makes you want to retreat farther inside the house to protect yourself against . . . a summer shower? Rationally, you know your reaction is ridiculous and that the shower will soon pass, but the distant rumble and occasional flashes still make your heart pound.

Symptoms of anxiety can be normal and expected responses much of the time (stress of a new job opportunity, fear of choking, danger from a severe storm), but they can also be debilitating and irrational (fear of inevitable failure resulting in catastrophe, inability even to look at a button, cowering in a gentle rainstorm). The preceding examples really demonstrate the difference between *fear* and *anxiety*. Although one might describe the feeling of being anxious as a feeling of "fear," fear is a response to a real threat (a hurricane), whereas anxiety is a response to a perceived threat (approaching rainstorm). Because it has a concrete and definite focus, fear usually recedes once the danger is removed. Anxiety, on the other hand, can feel as if it comes on for no apparent reason. In fact, it's hard to tell when anxiety begins and when it ends. It can be an all-consuming feeling of heightened vigilance surrounding something unknown that is yet to come, or the limitless aftershocks of going through a traumatic experience. The apparent lack of rhyme or reason is one of the things that make anxiety a debilitating emotion.

SYMPTOMS OF ANXIETY

Having defined what anxiety is, the next step is to familiarize yourself with its symptoms. Knowing how anxiety manifests itself is an important part of understanding the condition. If you know what to expect, not only can you manage anxiety in time, but you can also better anticipate—and therefore prevent and deal with—anxiety before it occurs. You will also be better able to communicate your situation to other people who can help.

The symptoms of anxiety can be divided into four slightly overlapping categories of symptoms: the physiological (what your body is experiencing), the cognitive (your thoughts), the emotional (your feelings), and the behavioral (what your body is doing externally).

Physiological Symptoms of Anxiety

Anxiety is not just a psychological phenomenon but a physical one as well. The experience of anxiety comes with specific changes in the body caused by what is commonly called the "fight-or-flight response." The rush of the hormones adrenaline, noradrenaline, and cortisol into the system stimulates the brain into a rapid assessment of the situation and prepares the body either to attack (fight) or to escape (flight) the cause of distress. (In some animals, another response is to freeze, perhaps best exemplified by the "deer in the headlights" reaction. The evolution of humans seems to have eliminated that response.)

"Acute stress response," also clinically known as "hyperarousal," is a theory put forth by Dr. Walter Cannon (1871–1945), an American, Harvard-educated physiologist. In short, Cannon described the body's natural response to a perceived threat.[1] Physiologically, the body responds in several ways, all designed to help you survive the threat before you. The release of hormones results in increased energy, a faster heart rate, slower digestion, and above-normal strength. Symptoms described as "heart pounding" or "frantic thinking" may also occur. More specifically, look for the following:

- Diarrhea, vomiting, and other gastric problems
- Frequent urination

- Flushing of the skin
- Light-headedness, headache
- Muscle tension
- Rapid heart rate and palpitation
- Recurrent, localized pain
- Shortness of breath
- Sleeping problems
- Sweating
- Tics (involuntary twitching of muscles)
- Tingling sensations

Cognitive Symptoms of Anxiety

The most common cognitive (mental) symptom is general worry or apprehension, most often about an anticipated event (rather than an occurring event) over which the person believes he or she has insufficient control. Worry need not be based on reality—as Cannon pointed out, it is *perceived* danger that causes the reaction, whether or not actual danger is present.[2] Other cognitive symptoms of anxiety include:

- A tendency to attribute negative events to personal traits
- Confusion, poor memory
- Decreased problem solving skills
- Difficulty concentrating, or paying and keeping attention
- Distortions in perception
- Morbid thoughts
- Obsessions
- Oversensitivity

Emotional Symptoms of Anxiety

Although emotional symptoms are in a way rooted in the physiological and cognitive symptoms, in the heat of the moment it is the emotional symptoms that are most obvious and in some ways, the most difficult to deal with. Many people suffering an attack of anxiety report the sense of having their emotions completely overtaking their mind and body, refusing to permit rational thought to regain control. Emotional symptoms of anxiety include:

- Anger, rage, lashing out
- Fear and even terror
- Fear of losing control
- Feeling as if one is not in one's body
- Feelings of apprehension
- Loss of sense of reality
- Panic; an extreme need to escape the situation

Behavioral Symptoms of Anxiety

The physiological symptoms of anxiety mostly affect the body internally, but the physiological, cognitive, and emotional symptoms together can affect one's outward behavior. It's perhaps for this reason that anxiety feels almost contagious: if someone is behaving differently or erratically because of anxiety, it can cause stress in others as well. Some more specific behavioral symptoms of anxiety include:

- Erratic behavior
- Failing to complete tasks, seeking easy tasks (avoiding challenge), or avoiding tasks altogether

- Fidgeting, hand wringing, finger tapping
- Irritability
- Perfectionism
- Pressured and rapid speech
- Restlessness, pacing, nervous shaking or moving of the limbs, trembling
- Withdrawal from people, lack of participation

You don't have to manifest all of these symptoms to call what you are feeling "anxiety." You may have a few of these symptoms, several of them, or something completely unique that nevertheless feels to you like unease or an "anxious feeling." You know yourself better than anyone, and despite medical science's best attempts to clearly define anxiety, you will likely find that the best gauge for your condition is still your own subjective experience.

Do you have trouble coping with what feels like an impending threat? If so, it's very likely that you are having anxious feelings. When consulting with a doctor or a therapist, you may find the preceding list of symptoms helpful in describing your feelings. Just remember that all of what you experience is important, so speak freely and honestly with the person you are consulting.

NORMAL VERSUS PATHOLOGICAL ANXIETY

We have discussed the idea that fear and anxiety are responses to a perceived threat, whether real or imagined. Does this mean that anxiety is, in a way, a normal response?

Strangely, the answer is yes. Anxiety, in and of itself, is an emotion as normal and regularly occurring as happiness, sadness, anger, or satisfaction. In fact, as we've already discussed, anxiety can be beneficial. When you are confronted by danger or a legitimate threat, the fight-or-flight response will help you realize that a full-grown black bear in the woods only *looks* cuddly and that it might be a better idea to give her and her cubs some space.

Some people find anxiety to be motivating. In school, they were those students who waited until the last minute, worked through the night, and produced an amazing paper just in time for class. Others seem to get creative only when they feel anxiety and pressure. As feminist writer Fay Weldon once said, "Deadlines and money—if I didn't have a deadline and never received payment, I wouldn't write at all!" For still others, anxiety is a comfort—they take it to mean that they are not being complacent and can still feel the appropriate emotion that accompanies a threat.

How, then, does anxiety become problematic?

When Anxiety Is No Longer Your Friend

There is an important difference between anxiety as an emotion and anxiety as a disorder. While the former is a temporary and normal reaction to threatening situations, the latter is a debilitating condition. Normally, three criteria must be met before you can consider a person's anxiety to be problematic: it must be *excessive*, *long-lasting*, and *interfering significantly with one's life*.

1. The problem is excessive. As we've seen, anxiety can be a normal emotional reaction to *stressors* (events that cause stress). Most of us are nervous about an appointment with a dentist, for example. However, if the thought of a dentist visit makes you so upset that you don't eat for a few days before the event, the reaction is excessive. A healthful fear of or respect for snakes is normal; being terrified even to look at a picture of a snake is excessive.

2. The problem is long-lasting. A general rule used by psychologists to define *long-lasting* is "the four-week rule." If the symptom(s) persists for four weeks or if symptoms recur within a four-week period, it may prompt a diagnosis of anxiety disorder. This is not an all-or-nothing rule; if you feel better after three weeks and six days, the diagnosis may still be accurate! A mental health professional will take many factors into consideration along with this four-week rule—it is only a guideline.

3. The problem interferes significantly with one's life. Anxiety can interfere with a person's work, relationships, and personal life. Pathological anxiety can prevent a person from being able to interact with others, making it difficult or impossible to hold down a job or to relate effectively with others. If the resulting distress and unease from the anxiety is enough to keep a person from accomplishing everyday tasks, then the anxiety is considered pathological.

These descriptions are general in nature, and you may feel that they apply to your situation to some degree but not specifically enough. Let's take a look at some of the types of anxiety disorders with the view of helping you understand your own situation more clearly.

TYPES OF ANXIETY DISORDERS

People experience anxiety differently. You may, for example, tend toward anxiety only during specific situations, like when you have to perform in public or be assessed by other people. Others may experience anxiety as a general fear of the unknown—they don't exactly know why they are apprehensive; all they know is that they feel uneasy about something. Still others feel anxious because they have gone through a life-threatening experience that they can't seem to shake.

If you understand what kind of anxiety you are dealing with, you can better plan ways to manage your condition. Although the categories may have some overlap between them, different kinds of anxiety have different dynamics. What's important is that you know which particular type of anxiety is troubling you so you can begin your research for a cure in the right direction.

The American Psychological Association (APA) has created a standardized manual for use in diagnosing a wide range of psychological issues, including the various forms of anxiety disorder. This manual is called the *Diagnostic and Statistical Manual of Mental Disorders* (*DSM*). It has been revised several times and is now in its fifth edition; the abbreviated title is *DSM-5*, and you may hear this abbreviation if you visit with a mental health professional.

The *DSM* describes each of the anxiety disorders that follow. Each description in the *DSM* includes criteria to be considered when assessing the presence of a mental health condition. We'll discuss these criteria generally. See how these descriptions may apply to you. In each description, you may find the three criteria already mentioned: *excessive, long-lasting*, and *interfering significantly with one's life.*

Generalized Anxiety Disorder (GAD)

Generalized anxiety disorder (GAD) is the most common of anxiety disorders; it affects about 3.1 percent of the U.S. population in a given year.[3] People suffering from GAD tend to live in a constant state of excessive worry and tension. Physical symptoms may include restlessness, fatigue, and difficulty falling asleep. Because of its pervasive effects, GAD is one of the most debilitating mental health conditions.

For reasons that may be biological or societal (or both), GAD occurs more frequently among women than among men. It often starts in the early teenage years and, if left untreated, progresses in intensity throughout life.

It's important to note that appropriate anxiety toward everyday stressors does not mean that a person has GAD. Instead, it is the constant worry—in spite of evidence that there is nothing to be anxious about—that makes GAD a disorder. If, for example, your spouse constantly assures you that you have the budget to pay your rent every month, yet still you ruminate every day about whether you're going to get evicted soon, then you may be suffering from GAD.

Panic Disorder (PD)

Almost everyone has experienced panic. When you realize that you left your garage door unlocked, you experience a moment of panic—what if your car is stolen or vandalized? When exam day finally arrives and you haven't mastered every lesson you were supposed to study, then you experience a moment of panic. The same goes when you're caught dipping your hands in the cookie jar but you're supposed to be on a diet.

The difference between panic and suffering from a panic disorder (PD) is the experience of frequent and intense panic attacks. A panic attack is a period of extreme tension and anxiety, usually lasting for ten to fifteen minutes; it can be so severe that you quite literally feel you are about to die (a choking feeling, heart palpitations, etc.). A panic attack can be brought on by a specific trigger (such as a threatening thought or situation), or it can come on seemingly without cause. People with PD experience several panic attacks over a comparatively short period of time. (You may recall the "four-week rule" discussed earlier.)

Common symptoms of a panic attack include:

- Fast heart rate (tachycardia or palpitations)
- Fear of losing control
- Feeling detachment from one's body
- Nausea, dizziness, stomach upset
- Shortness of breath, perhaps even a feeling of being choked or strangled

It is believed that about 2 percent of the U.S. population suffers from PD. Like GAD, PD affects women more than men. The condition is commonly accompanied by agoraphobia (to be discussed next) as well as the avoidance of situations that trigger an anxiety attack. Symptoms of panic attacks are similar to many other medical conditions, which is why PD tends to be misdiagnosed or underdiagnosed by general medical practitioners.[4]

Agoraphobia

Agoraphobia is an irrational fear of being out in public and can be found in as much as 50 percent of all cases of people with PD.[5] The name comes from a Greek phrase meaning "fear of the marketplace." The main characteristic of agoraphobia is anxiety when in places where escape is difficult or awkward (e.g., a party or the middle of a stadium during a football match) or in situations where help is hard to come by. Extreme agoraphobics often remain completely housebound—living in fear of leaving their own home.

Agoraphobia is the most common type of phobia, affecting an estimated 5 to 12 percent of the U.S. population during their lifetime. Agoraphobia occurs twice as often in women as in men and typically affects people between the ages of fifteen and thirty-five.[6]

Specific Phobias

Have you ever met a person who has an extreme fear of heights? Stepping onto a balcony would probably cause her to break out in a sweat. Or perhaps you've met someone who has an irrational fear of spiders. Fearing large, poisonous spiders is, of course, normal, but this person shakes at the sight of any small, harmless eight-legged creature. Even toy spiders or pictures of a spider might make the person feel afraid. These people suffer from specific phobias.

Specific phobias refer to intense and generally irrational fears of specific objects or situations to a degree out of proportion with the actual threat the object or situation poses. The term *phobia* stems from a character in Greek mythology named Phobos—son of Ares, the god of war—who was so terrifying that people lay panicking at his feet. Thus one characteristic of specific phobias is extreme, debilitating fear. More often than not, persons suffering from a phobia know that their reaction is exaggerated—however, they still can't help it.

There are four basic subtypes of specific phobias: natural environment (e.g., fear of thunder or lightning), animals (e.g., fear of cats or dogs), situations (e.g., fear of public speaking or meeting new people), and blood, injections, and injury (e.g., the fear of taking an X-ray or undergoing a root canal).

Examples of specific phobias include:

- Arachnophobia—fear of spiders
- Bathmophobia—fear of stairs
- Belonephobia—fear of needles
- Brontophobia—fear of thunder
- Claustrophobia—fear of closed spaces
- Ophidiophobia—fear of snakes
- Ornithophobia—fear of birds
- Pediophobia—fear of dolls
- Triskaidekaphobia—fear of the number thirteen
- Xenophobia—fear of strangers

It is estimated that 11 percent of the general population has some form of specific phobia, but not everyone with these conditions seeks professional treatment.[7] Compared with other anxiety disorders, specific phobias may not cause significant impairment to a person's work or relational life. In general, as long as the object of one's phobia is avoided or anticipated, a person can live a full, healthy life.

Obsessive-Compulsive Disorder (OCD)

If you're a fan of popular culture, chances are you've heard of obsessive-compulsive disorder (OCD). From Adrian Monk—the obsessive-compulsive detective in the TV series *Monk*—to Jack Nicholson's annoying yet endearing character in the motion picture *As Good as It Gets,* many fictional accounts of OCD can be found on TV and in film. What often is not shown, however, is the extreme difficulty people with OCD experience with their condition. While symptoms of OCD may seem funny or amusing to onlookers, they bring strong feelings of anxiety to the person experiencing them.

Let's begin with a definition. First, what are obsessions? Obsessions refer to unwanted, persistently distressing thoughts about a particular subject matter. Anything can be an object of an obsession, and although a person may try to suppress these thoughts, it is often to no avail. You may, for example, obsess about being at the top of your class and think about achieving first place above other priorities. Or you may obsess about cleanliness—constantly worrying whether the dinner the waitress served you was cooked in a sterile kitchen or whether you're catching germs from your seatmate on the train. You might even obsess about a particular person, such as an ex-lover or a celebrity.

Obsessions are thoughts, whereas compulsions are repetitive behaviors exhibited to relieve the anxiety caused by obsessions. If you obsess about being first in your class, for example, you may annoyingly check every test paper of your classmates to verify that you indeed have the highest marks. If you obsess about safety, you may tend to check and double-check whether you've locked your doors for the night. If you obsess about neatness, you may be rigid about the way you arrange your shelves or drawers, and feel anxious if even one item is out of place. Checking compulsions are more common among men, and washing compulsions are more common among women.

Every person is obsessive-compulsive to some degree, and just because you may have obsessive-compulsive traits doesn't mean you have OCD. The measure of having OCD is the degree to which you have obsessions and compulsions, and to what extent they may interfere with your quality of life. Obsessions in OCD are irrational—that is, there is no logical reason to think constantly about your obsession, and yet you still do. You may, for example, have taken every possible step to sterilize your home, and still obsess about the germs on the tiles. Obsession may cause anxiety, especially when you are prevented from acting out the compulsive behavior designed to alleviate the obsessive symptom. Ultimately, performing the compulsive action brings only temporary relief; the person with true OCD will find that the cycle persists and repeats itself after some short period of time.

Social Anxiety Disorder (SAD)

Also known as "social phobia," social anxiety disorder (SAD) refers to an intense, long-lasting fear of social situations or situations perceived to be scrutinized by other people. It is different than shyness or introversion because people with SAD experience extreme anxiety simply at the thought of interacting with other people; they feel so uncomfortable in social situations that they often just avoid them.

Some people with SAD experience anxiety over only specific social situations. For example, there are people who fear introducing themselves to strangers but are otherwise fine interacting with people, and the most common form of SAD is the fear of public speaking. There are also people who fear eating in public places, like in restaurants or at parties. There are still others who experience social anxiety more broadly—they fear all kinds of situations where there are other people. Because some degree of social interaction is important for one's personal and professional growth, SAD at its most extreme can result in significant impairment in quality of life.

It is estimated that 4 percent of adults in the United States show symptoms of SAD. Again, perhaps because of changing social expectations, SAD is twice as common in women as in men. Research shows that male sufferers tend to seek professional help for their condition more than women, again perhaps because of the social expectations of men to excel in their professions.[8]

Acute Stress Disorder (ASD)

There are occasions when anxiety symptoms come as a result of a traumatic event. For time-limited anxious reactions that result from a perceived threat, the diagnosis given is acute stress disorder (ASD).

Acute stress disorder is caused by exposure to trauma or situations that place severe stress on a person. What can be considered traumatic differs from person to person, but there are events that are typically considered traumatic. The death of a loved one, witnessing or being a victim of violence, experiencing a natural or man-made disaster, and participating in combat can all be considered traumatic for a person.

Symptoms of ASD include avoidance of reminders of the traumatic event; stress symptoms such as irritability, poor concentration, and health issues; unwanted reexperiencing of the trauma; hypervigilance; and extreme psychological arousal and anxiety when faced with reminders of the difficult time.

Acute stress disorder may also include depersonalization and derealization. *Depersonalization* refers to the feeling that one's body is unreal, changing, or dissolving. *Derealization*, on the other hand, refers to the feeling that one's external environment is unreal. ASD typically appears within one month of exposure to traumatic events and usually goes away in one to two months.

Post-Traumatic Stress Disorder (PTSD)

Acute stress disorder is a time-limited anxiety reaction to a traumatic event—the symptoms appear for a while and then quickly disappear. If anxiety symptoms from a traumatic event persist for more than three months, the diagnosis given is post-traumatic stress disorder (PTSD).

Post-traumatic stress disorder has become part of our daily culture as a result of warriors returning from combat. In World War I, the term commonly used was *shell shock*; in World War II, the term *battle fatigue* came into use. When the syndrome was studied more carefully after the Vietnam War, the APA derived the descriptive term *post-traumatic stress disorder*, widening the definition to include not merely wartime trauma but also events such as plane crashes, natural disasters, and other extreme experiences.

The risk of PTSD is strongest among women forty to sixty years old with little to no experience of coping with traumatic events. Although exposure to trauma occurs to as much as 70 percent of the population, PTSD has a lifetime prevalence of 7 to 9 percent of the general population.[9]

A Word of Caution

It is important to emphasize that only a licensed mental health practitioner can diagnose an anxiety disorder accurately. Diagnosing anxiety is complex—there are many possible causes behind the symptoms of anxiety, and anxiety has different forms. For this reason, it is always advisable to seek the opinion of a professional instead of self-diagnosing your anxiety condition. These descriptions may help you explain and describe your own experience of your symptoms to your physician or mental health practitioner.

Now that you've learned the basics of defining anxiety, and taken a good look at the symptoms and types, it's time to move on to see where exactly anxiety comes from.

Understand the Roots and Causes of Anxiety and Related Conditions

When you're in the middle of an anxiety attack, it's hard to pin down the exact cause of your worry and apprehension; anxiety can be overwhelming, to the degree that it pushes away rational thought. If you are able to think clearly enough to take what is called a "metaposition"—to look at your anxiety from a third-person point of view—you'll find that likely a combination of factors makes you prone to anxiety.

ROOTS AND CAUSES OF ANXIETY

Some of the roots of anxiety may even stem from as early as your childhood. Understanding where your anxiety comes from is an important part of the journey to overcome your anxiety. Consider the following possible causes of anxiety.

Genes

Although it's difficult to conceptualize feelings as hereditary, research findings show that the tendency toward anxiety is something that runs in families. Children with anxiety disorders are likely to have parents with anxiety disorders, and vice versa. Siblings also tend to share anxiety disorders. Perhaps the most revealing research was performed on identical twins separated at birth and raised separately; studies showed that if one twin has an anxiety disorder, the other twin will very likely have it as well.[10]

In some ways, knowing that your anxiety is genetic can be comforting. Being genetically predisposed to anxiety means that you can't rationally blame yourself for the difficulty that you are experiencing. Knowing that anxiety runs in families can also help you better anticipate anxiety attacks. If you know that you come from a family that is prone to anxiety, you can start learning early the anxiety management techniques that, can help you better cope with your condition. You can also become more aware that compared with the general population, you have to work harder at keeping your anxiety under control.

Upbringing

Research into anxious children reveals that kids prone to anxiety often describe their parents as overprotective, ambivalent, rejecting, and hostile. Similarly, adults with anxiety disorders refer to their parents as controlling and lacking in affection. These findings suggest that high levels of anxiety may be correlated to the child-rearing style of one's parents.

It's easy to deduce why parental overprotectiveness might be a factor in a child developing anxiety. If you don't get to try out many activities—activities where there's a chance you would get defeated or rejected—then there's less room for you to develop your emotional coping muscles in preparation for these types of situations. If you're never allowed to play sports with your peers, for example, you may not learn your actual competencies, and this lack of knowledge can translate into performance anxiety. If you're not allowed to make friends, you won't learn what it feels like to adjust to different people, hence making you anxious in social situations. Overprotective parents don't realize it, but they are likely to actually do their children more harm than good.

Similarly, distant or rejecting parents can create anxiety in their children because they set a certain expectation of negativity. Some years ago, when the description of the Type A personality came into general public awareness, these highly driven, success-oriented people were often discovered to have had parents who would severely punish the slightest disappointments (e.g., a report card with even a single B grade on it), while extraordinary success (e.g., winning a statewide report-writing competition) was met with indifference, if it was acknowledged at all.

Remember that parents are the first people whose opinions matter to a child, and if one can't please one's parents, there's a good chance that a person will never develop a healthy sense of self. Rejection also makes a child feel as if he or she is not a person of worth, which can in turn result in many other negative emotions.

Negative Past Experiences

Anxiety can be a learned reaction to something that has proven to be threatening in the past. Consider a situation where you had little to no control—a situation that resulted in serious negative consequences, whether emotional (acute embarrassment) or physical (serious injury). There's no doubt that the traumatic event caused anxiety; however, it's also likely that encountering a similar situation may revive or even amplify that anxiety later in life.

A child who has almost drowned, for example, may develop anxious feelings every time he is near a swimming pool. A person who has been embarrassed in public may develop a fear of open spaces or crowds of unfamiliar people. Similarly, a person who has experienced a robbery with violence may develop a fear of people who might resemble the original attacker(s) or be anxious in any situation that highlights one's weakness.

Of course, not everyone who has encountered a negative experience develops further anxiety after the event. It depends on the person's coping resources during and soon after the time of the negative event. A person who is generally resilient is less likely to be conditioned toward fear and anxiety than someone who has poor coping mechanisms and little emotional support.

Chronic Exposure to Upsetting Stimuli

A person's environment can have a strong influence on his or her level of anxiety. If you are in a workplace that is stressful, for example, there is a good chance that concentration and focus can be difficult. Combine this difficulty with everyday deadlines or particularly high-pressure situations, and it can easily trigger anxiety. If the home you live in is in need of numerous repairs, you may never feel safe enough to relax, and this can also trigger anxiety. The same goes if you live in a neighborhood known for its high crime rate.

Some environmental conditions known to increase anxiety include loud noises, bright lights, and chemical vapors. If you are also constantly exposed to distressing news—such as news of violence and unrest on television—you are more likely to develop anxiety. Similarly, repeated exposure to other anxious people can increase the level of one's anxiety.

The increased pace of daily life in the United States is in itself a contributor to stress and anxiety. In today's world of instant messaging, smart phones, twenty-four-hour news channels, tweets, and social networking, we are constantly bombarded with information, starving for knowledge, and largely overstimulated. Everything seems to require our attention, all at the same time, resulting in the rise of multitasking—a term originally created to describe how a computer accomplishes multiple tasks and runs multiple processes simultaneously. Just like computers, humans can become overloaded with too much input. Unlike computers, however, humans can't simply "reboot" after a crash and become healthy again; we are complex in ways that computers are not, and we need other means of dealing with our stressful overloads.

Stressful Life Events

A person can encounter many stressful events over the course of a lifetime that can result in anxious feelings. Some even have happy aspects (e.g., marriage, the birth of a child, a special birthday or anniversary), while many others may not (e.g., a death in the family, loss of a job, loss of a family pet). Whether planned for or discovered accidentally, whether necessary or voluntary, large changes in our lives can create stress and anxiety.

As is the case with other potential causes of anxiety, the amount of anxiety any individual person feels during stressful life events depends on that person's coping resources. Some people would find going to college stressful, for example, whereas others would consider it a breeze. In general, any situation that brings about a loss of some kind can be a trigger for anxiety. The stress can also be aggravated if the person feels little to no control over the situation that brings about the loss.

Repressed Emotions

There is a school of psychology called "psychoanalysis" (pioneered by Sigmund Freud and his student Carl Jung), which asserts that anxiety conditions are brought about by emotions that a person has tried to bury (repress) in his subconscious mind. In other words, psychoanalysis says that if you don't allow yourself to fully feel what may be considered socially unacceptable emotions, there is a good chance that your real feelings will play out during anxiety-provoking situations. Repressed anger is the emotion most associated with anxiety disorders, but it's certainly not the only one.

Take the case of a person who experiences extreme anxiety regarding cleanliness and feels compelled to wash his or her hands several times a day just to feel clean. From the standpoint of psychoanalysis, this person would be expressing this compulsion because of an unacknowledged feeling of being a "dirty" person or of having done something that causes great shame and anger. You may recall Shakespeare's portrayal of the sleepwalking Lady Macbeth, trying to wash her hands clean of the blood she had caused to be spilled (the source of the oft-quoted phrase, "Out, damned spot!").

The discovery and exploration of repressed emotions takes a great deal of time as well as the help and guidance of a skilled mental health professional. If you would like to discover whether your anxiety is subconscious in origin, it's best to find a licensed professional who specializes in psychoanalysis. Note, however, that you don't always have to know the subconscious origins of your anxiety to deal with it effectively. As long as you can apply known, effective techniques in managing anxiety, it is possible to lower your anxiety levels to a significant degree.

Irrational Thinking

As mentioned earlier, anxiety is caused by perception—it's what you think and feel about a particular event, person, or situation that triggers anxiety surrounding it. Imagine a large dog approaching you, trotting up slowly, his tail wagging. If you've had positive or even neutral encounters with large dogs, you might smile, or even reach out to hug or pet him. If you've had negative encounters with large dogs (or any dogs, for that matter), instead of possibly interacting with the dog and its owner, you are much more likely to be anxious, nervous, or uncertain as he approaches. The dog is the same dog in both instances; however, it's your perception, colored by your past experience, that makes the difference. The good news here is that with practice and increasing awareness of your own anxiety triggers, you can *choose* (make the rational choice) to interpret the event as neutral or even positive; over time, this way of thinking and reacting may lower your anxiety or perhaps even eliminate it in similar instances.

Slippery-slope thinking is a type of logical fallacy that assumes that if A happens, it will necessarily cause B, which will then necessarily cause C, and so on, each result bringing with it a greater catastrophe than the one before. Starting with something as foolish as pushing the wrong button in the elevator, one might imagine a string of events resulting in the entire state being swallowed whole by an earthquake. Imagining the end of the world being ultimately caused simply by pushing an elevator button would probably stop most of us from pushing that button. It doesn't matter that the idea is irrational or objectively ridiculous; as we've discussed before, anxiety can be overwhelming and often pushes the rational mind aside with great force. Once again, however, it's fully possible to reclaim your rational mind and instead push aside the anxiety, which frees you to push any elevator button you wish.

Poor Self-Esteem

Self-esteem refers to the way in which you regard yourself. If you think of yourself as capable, intelligent, affable, and trustworthy, then you have a healthy or high self-esteem. Conversely, if you consider yourself unworthy of people's warm regard or generally good for nothing, then you are suffering from low or poor self-esteem.

Unhealthy self-esteem is a leading cause of anxiety disorders. If you have a poor sense of self, you are more likely to give in to your insecurities instead of tackling your problems head on. You are also more likely to be pessimistic, perhaps resulting in poor action (or no action), which in turn leads to more anxiety. There are many different reasons why a person may have self-esteem problems, and exploring them with the help of a licensed professional can give your rational mind a leg up the next time you find yourself wrapped in self-doubt.

Medical Conditions that Mimic Anxiety

Because there is a physiological component to anxiety, it's also important to check whether your anxiety is being caused or made worse by specific medical conditions that you may have. Many medical conditions mimic anxiety—that is, when you experience these conditions, you feel as if you're having an anxiety attack but you actually aren't. Treating the medical condition may reduce the frequency or intensity of such attacks, while failing to treat the underlying condition may result in more, and more frequent, attacks.

Medical conditions that can mimic anxiety include:

Hyperthyroidism. The condition where the thyroid glands produce an excessive amount of thyroid hormones that circulate in the blood is hyperthyroidism. Patients with mild versions of the disease don't experience any symptoms, but severe hyperthyroidism can result in excessive sweating, tremors, nervousness and agitation, rapid heart rate, poor concentration, and weight loss. People with hyperthyroidism tend toward anxiety because their symptoms predispose them to feeling apprehension about even minor events.

Hyperventilation Syndrome. The respiratory ailment characterized by breathing too deeply or too rapidly is known as hyperventilation syndrome (HVS). It can be caused by physical and psychological conditions. People with HVS tend to experience chest pain, dizziness, a tingling sensation in their fingertips and mouth, and difficulty breathing. Panic attacks are usually accompanied by HVS.

Hypoglycemia. Also known as low blood sugar, hypoglycemia occurs when the glucose content in the blood drops below normal levels. It often happens suddenly, which is why a hypoglycemic attack is often mistaken for a panic attack. Symptoms of hypoglycemia include low energy, confusion, clumsiness, and fainting. Severe hypoglycemia can result in a coma, and in extreme cases, even death.

The good news is that hypoglycemia is easy to treat. Find food that is rich in glucose (e.g., candy or fruit juice) or starch (e.g., bread, crackers, potatoes). After you've had these foods to get sugar into your system quickly, it's strongly recommended to eat some foods more rich in protein (e.g., meat, eggs, cheese), which will break down more slowly. This will prevent a "rebound" effect—another more severe crash after the first crash has been dealt with.

Mitral valve prolapse. Also known as "click murmur syndrome" and "Barlow's syndrome," mitral valve prolapse is a heart valve abnormality. It is hereditary and is estimated to affect 2 to 3 percent of the world's population.[11] Its exact cause is still being investigated; risk factors may include having had rheumatic fever or having too low a body mass index (BMI). People suffering from mitral valve prolapse report symptoms such as fatigue, palpitations, chest pain, difficulty breathing, and migraine headaches. It is a condition commonly associated with anxiety, panic attacks, and depression.

Premenstrual syndrome. For women, anxiety issues appear to be a common occurrence during changes in the hormonal cycle.

Emotional symptoms vary from woman to woman, but some report extreme emotionality, crying spells, feelings of impending doom, and general unease when they are about to get their monthly period. Some women who are prone to anxiety episodes report that their symptoms are generally worse during certain parts of their menstrual cycle than others.

Drug Side Effects

If you're prone to anxiety, you might want to check with your doctor to see if your medications have anxiety-like symptoms as a side effect. Known medications that cause anxiety include local anesthetics, birth control pills, some thyroid or asthma drugs, antihypertensive medications, corticosteroids, nonsteroidal anti-inflammatory drugs (NSAIDs), and some psychotropic agents (drugs prescribed for mental illness, such as Prozac, Sinequan, and Zoloft). Withdrawal from some prescription drugs, such as beta-blockers and corticosteroids, can also result in anxiety-like symptoms. The same goes for withdrawal from commonly abused drugs, such as alcohol, cocaine, and opiates.

If you think a medication you are on is contributing to your feelings of anxiety, consult your doctor or pharmacist, or visit the Physicians' Desk Reference website (PDR.net) for more complete information.

COMMON MENTAL HEALTH CONDITIONS ASSOCIATED WITH ANXIETY

It's important to know that sometimes anxiety does not come alone. There are occasions when anxiety manifests itself alongside other mental health conditions, which makes diagnosis and treatment a little bit trickier. Knowing which conditions are commonly associated with anxiety can help you arm yourself against a possible worsening of your disease.

A number of mental health conditions are frequently associated with anxiety, and here are some of the most common.

Depression

Research has found that anxiety often precedes the onset of mood disorders, particularly major depressive disorder (MDD). People who experience anxiety have also been found to experience more severe and long-lasting depression, sometimes accompanied by hospitalization, suicidal thoughts, and marked impairment in functioning. It is important, then, to arrest anxiety disorders early so they will not progress into this more serious mental illness.

Major depressive disorder, or recurrent depressive disorder, is characterized by an all-encompassing low mood accompanied by self-hatred and lack of interest in activities usually found to be pleasurable. Major depressive disorder is different from the normal sadness that accompanies negative life experiences. Instead, it is more pervasive and affects a person's everyday life. In the United States an estimated 3.5 percent of the people with MDD attempt suicide. Major depressive disorder is most commonly associated with generalized anxiety disorder (GAD) and panic disorder (PD).[12]

Substance Abuse

Anxiety is also commonly associated with substance use and abuse. For instance, nearly 30 percent of people with PD use alcohol to self-medicate their anxiety. Although alcohol can help alleviate the symptoms of a panic attack in the short term, over time alcohol does more harm than good. The symptoms of panic attacks actually get worse after the effects of the drug have worn off. Further, the use of alcohol may interfere with work, relationships, and other social interactions, which often promotes a downward spiral of anxiety. If you are struggling with substance abuse and think it might be contributing to your feelings of anxiety, talk to your doctor or seek other professional help.

Other Mental Health Conditions

Certain other mental health conditions have become a common topic of conversation because of new research, new diagnostic tools, and greater exposure in the mainstream media. It is important to note that the common discussion of these conditions does not mean that more cases are occurring than before, only that older, incorrect diagnoses are now being corrected and properly treated. It is less likely that you have these conditions; however, their prevalence in the media may cause you to consider them. Regardless of prevalence, these conditions are also often associated with feelings of anxiety.

Asperger's syndrome. A form of high-functioning autism, Asperger's syndrome (AS) is characterized by significant difficulties in social interaction and in nonverbal communication.

Someone with AS may have an intense fascination with a particular subject (a mild form of monomania) as well as restrictive and repetitive patterns of behavior and interest. Not unlike the ways particular obsessions and compulsions associated with obsessive-compulsive disorder (OCD) can be anxiety inducing, the monomania and types of behavioral patterns that can accompany AS can also bring about anxious feelings. Because of its lack of distinctive symptomology (in other words, distinct from other syndromes in the spectrum of symptoms included under the category of autism spectrum disorder), AS was actually dropped as a specific diagnosis in the fifth edition of the *Diagnostic and Statistical Manual (DSM)* of the American Psychological Association. Many people still stand by older diagnostic categories, and the full impact of this reclassification is yet to be fully understood or felt.

Tourette's syndrome. An inherited neuropsychiatric disorder characterized by multiple physical (motor) tics and at least one vocal (phonic) tic, Tourette's syndrome (TS) is most often diagnosed during childhood. The most publicized symptom—and interestingly, the least often manifested—is coprolalia, the spontaneous utterance of socially objectionable or taboo words or phrases. Simply worrying that one might suddenly shout out an obscenity, for no reason, in a public place is quite enough to cause stress and anxiety, which itself can trigger coprolalia and exacerbate other TS symptoms.

These first two steps have explored the causes and nature of anxiety. From the environment in which people are brought up to their unique life experiences and individual genetic makeup, anxiety has its roots in many different places. While the symptoms of a number of conditions can mimic those of anxiety disorders, others are strongly associated with and can even exacer-bate feelings of anxiety. With a better understanding of the many contributing factors, the next step is to think about ways to man-age anxiety, even when it seems the least manageable.

Managing Anxiety

STEP 3
Find Some Instant Calm

STEP 4
Get in Tune with Your Thoughts and Feelings

STEP 5
Develop Behavioral Techniques and Mental Strategies

....

This section will present you with an array of tools that you can use to manage the debilitating feelings that come from anxiety. You are free to pick just one method to faithfully follow, or mix and match the different techniques to create an anxiety management plan tailor-made for your needs. For best results, align the anxiety treatment of your choice with the cause of your anxiety.

Find Some Instant Calm

One of the most debilitating problems with anxiety disorders is their ability to build in intensity. For example, say you're on your way to a job interview, and you get a flat tire. The action of changing a flat tire can be simple enough, as is calling the person you were going to meet with to explain why you're running late; however, anxiety can push your rational thoughts out of the way and direct you to more catastrophic ones (the "slippery slope" discussed earlier): this delay will cause you to be late to your job interview, they'll count that against you and not hire you, you'll fail at ever getting any job ever again, and you'll lose your home and be a loser for the rest of your life! Or what if you want to express a small complaint to your spouse? It will definitely be interpreted incorrectly, your spouse will leave you, there will be an ugly divorce, and you'll become a laughingstock, despised by everyone! When anxiety is in the driver's seat, it's all too easy for it to drive you and your rational mind right over the cliff.

Managing anxiety has two distinct processes: long term and short term. In the long term, coming to understand the roots of your particular anxiety will help you diminish and lessen the anxiety attacks that you may experience. However, that can take a long time, and anxiety attacks are very much part of the "now." In the present moment, the goal is to calm yourself quickly—to let your rational mind regain control of the runaway thoughts and fears exacerbated by the anxiety attack.

WAYS TO FIND INSTANT CALM

Anxiety is considered to be the number one mental health condition in existence, affecting as many as fifty million Americans a year. This estimate may even be conservative, because many people with anxiety do not go to their physician or mental health professional to be diagnosed properly. It is believed that anxiety costs the nation billions of dollars a year in lost work and damaged or destroyed relationships.

The good news is that anxiety is a treatable disorder. There are many things that you can do to get immediate relief from this debilitating condition. The "trick" to finding calm in the midst of an anxiety attack is to put your mind back in charge of the moment. Anxiety triggers physiological responses—rapid heartbeat, labored breathing, increased blood pressure, and any number of the fight-or-flight responses. Just as your mind (your perception) has made this happen, so can it reverse its negative effects. Since so many people suffer from different variations of anxiety with many different causes, and since not everyone responds to the same management strategies, there are many things you can do to lessen your anxiety.

The following are just some of the strategies you can use to counteract the effects of an anxiety attack.

Self-Talk

Whenever you feel an anxiety attack coming on, it helps to give yourself an empowering and encouraging talk. To prevent yourself from being overwhelmed by what you're feeling, you can also debate with that voice in your head encouraging you to panic—let the more assertive side of your personality take control. It could also help to whisper soothing words to yourself as you wait for your breathing and your heart rate to return to normal.

Some examples of self-talk include:

- "Everything is going to be okay."
- "This is just one incident—it doesn't define me."
- "You can handle this; just take it one day at a time."
- "This is not as bad as it seems."
- "You've been through this before; you can get through it again."

Breathing Exercises

Another way to instantly calm yourself is through breathing exercises. The simplest of these exercises is to inhale slowly, hold your breath for a slow count of five, and then release the breath slowly. To make it more effective, inhale through the nose, hold, and then exhale through a pursed mouth, as if you were blowing up a balloon. (You'll notice that the exhale can take a while this way; don't worry, that's exactly what it's supposed to do.)

You may also use breathing exercises from Eastern meditation techniques such as yoga and tai chi (discussed later). If you were to take just one point from these meditative techniques, you should focus on the chest as you inhale and exhale. You should be able to feel the chest expanding fully during the inhale and contracting again while exhaling. At its simplest level, this focus will help distract your mind still further from whatever might be causing the anxiety attack.

In more extreme cases, physical symptoms of anxiety can include hyperventilation (too much oxygen in the blood), rapid heart rate, and elevated blood pressure. These symptoms can make you feel as if there's a heavy weight on your chest, steel bars in your lungs, or both. To help manage these symptoms, you may also try breathing in and out of a clean paper bag. The porous bag will let some air in, but the majority of the air you are breathing will consist of carbon dioxide; this will help lower the level of oxygen in your blood, which will help make you feel more calm. If you begin to feel dizzy, stop using the bag and breathe normally.

Just remember: the bag must be made of paper! Breathing through a plastic bag could result in suffocation.

Guided Imagery

When you feel like an anxiety attack is about to come on, it can be helpful to imagine a place or a situation that you find peaceful and calming. For example, imagine that you're on a secluded beach or a mountaintop, away from the worries of the world, or imagine that you are enveloped in a bubble of safety and no anxiety trigger can touch you while you're in your place of solace. You can also try bringing to mind a happy memory—like your first kiss, a big win, your wedding day, or the first time you held your child. Transporting yourself to these places and times—even temporarily—can help you get a handle on the situation you're having difficulty dealing with. This has become known colloquially as "going to your happy place."

For best results, engage all your senses whenever you're conducting a visualization exercise. You can, for example, imagine how a tranquil sea would sound and smell, or picture the colors present in a beautiful sunset or sunrise. The more vivid a picture you can make, the better your chances of finding instant calm in it.

Prayer or Meditation

If you're religious, you might consider prayer as a possible way of experiencing instant calm. Research has shown that prayer is an effective way of soothing many negative moods, especially if the prayer involves surrender of one's situation to a higher power. You can include in your prayer a specific petition for managing your anxiety better.

If you have a specifically worded prayer in mind, perhaps the Serenity Prayer, the Lord's Prayer, or the Twenty-third Psalm, be careful not to rush through the words. Bring each word to your mind as if you've never said it before, or as if you were writing it down on paper. This, too, will help shift the focus of your thoughts from the cause of the anxiety to the more rational mind, giving you the chance to bring your rational mind back into focus.

If you're not exactly one for prayer but are looking for a similar experience, you might try some simple meditation—one of many techniques focusing on one's inner self to achieve an altered state of consciousness. There are many ways to meditate. Some people meditate by repeating a mantra such as "om" over and over again; others meditate through physical exercises such as yoga or tai chi; and many also find that simply sitting in contemplative silence is effective.

Meditation is often successful because of the many cognitive symptoms of anxiety. When your mind is racing with many jumbled thoughts, a focusing exercise can really cut to the core of whatever it is that might be causing anxiety. Meditation can also promote mindful living—being fully conscious of what you are doing—and lessen the mind's reaction to stress.

Gratitude

The expression "count your blessings" may sound cliché, but it's one way to bring greater calm to your mind. People have a tendency to think of only the negative things during moments of extreme anxiety. Think instead about everything that you have to be thankful for, and look for what is right in the world. The more entries that you can put on your gratitude list, the better off you'll be, and the more conscious an effort you make to practice gratitude in your daily life, the easier it will become.

Water

Water is an instant refresher, so make sure you always have a glass handy whenever you're faced with an anxiety-provoking situation. Water therapy is also good for the long-term management of stress and anxiety. Drinking water detoxifies your body—it helps the kidneys better process everything from toxins to excess sugar in your bloodstream. Remember also that to work best, water should be simply water, not the water found in coffee, tea, soda, or the "enhanced" waters that may contain anything from vitamins to caffeine. If the water from the tap doesn't taste good to you, add ice or consider getting some kind of water filter. Don't be concerned about needing to make more trips to the bathroom; it's a good way to take a five-minute break from your stress-causing activities.

Exercise

Stress and anxiety create physiological responses—the body feels attacked, and the fight-or-flight response kicks in. Thus, when faced with a threatening event, anxiety is felt because the body is getting ready for immediate action. Although immediate action was the norm in many older societies, the current state of civilization doesn't always allow one to physically act out tension. It's not likely that you will need to flee from a saber-toothed tiger, and it's not work appropriate to leap across the aisle to slap a nasty office-mate upside the head. You will need to find more socially acceptable ways of expending the energy that comes from the fight-or-flight response.

In the absence of fleeing a carnivorous predator, how can you dispel all that energy and adrenaline when your body says "panic!" for seemingly no reason? Exercise. Run a few laps, take a brisk walk around the office building, or do some push-ups. If you can channel all the energy from the fight-or-flight response into a socially acceptable form of physical exertion, you can often come down in no time. It may be time to reconsider that gym membership offer.

This tip has hidden benefits. It should be noted that exercise will help tone the body, lowering overall blood pressure levels; clearing toxins from the muscles, blood, and lymphatic system; and improving the heart rate—all things that will make the physiological effects of a panic attack less severe. We'll talk more about the long-term benefits of taking up some regular exercise later.

When you have finished exercising (or simply as an activity on its own), you might try dousing the fight-or-flight flames with a cold shower. The sudden dip in temperature can make you more conscious of your surroundings and be helpful in terms of putting your rational mind back in control.

Uplifting, Inspirational, or Relaxing Music

Mindlab International, a research company based in the United Kingdom, has found that listening to upbeat songs can get your pulse racing—and make you feel good the whole day. The best soundtracks for a smile-filled day, as common experience suggests, include "Dancing Queen" by ABBA, "Jump" by Van Halen, and "Greatest Day" by Take That. But you can customize your playlist according to your musical tastes, of course.

Music in general is a great regulator of mood, and happy music—any music with a catchy beat and positive words—is a great way to lessen anxiety. So pick up your favorite inspirational tune and have it handy in your iPod or MP3 player. If the song is catchy enough that it can make you dance, then you have the bonus of also being able to dance your cares away. And we've already talked about the benefits of exercise.

A different but related musical strategy involves drowning your anxieties and the world in ambient noises or the relaxing instrumental music of your favorite artists. Close your eyes, and listen intently; focus on the differences in every sound and every note. Quiet music can lull you into a state of calm and relaxation— which is perfect if you're struggling to keep things under control. Classical music such as Debussy's *Clair de Lune* or Beethoven's *Pastorale* can soothe; look also for music described as "ambient," with soft, slow, and soothing patterns of instrumental or electronic music.

Finding the Humor

Mother Teresa, renowned for her work with the poor, ill, and abandoned of Calcutta, was once asked how she dealt with so much hardship in her life. "I know that God would not give me more than I can handle," she said firmly, then added, with a smile, "Sometimes, I wish that He wouldn't trust me so much!"[13]

Humor is always a good way to release tension, and it really wouldn't hurt to laugh once in a while! Even disastrous moments can have their share of funny bits; you just need to be open to the opportunity for laughter. Having a sense of humor is actually the best cure for people suffering from obsessions and compulsions. Something in the situation is very likely to be funny, or at least to remind you of something funny, and if you can laugh at how ridiculous and irrational your response is, you are already well on your way to getting better.

Norman Cousins, for example, became famous (in part) by laughing himself back to health. Diagnosed with a presumably terminal disease that was to take his life inside of six months, Cousins simply refused to give in and went on to live nearly twenty years longer.[14] His greatest self-treatment was to watch films by the comic greats like the Marx Brothers; a good belly laugh, he said, could give him a full two hours without pain. Build your own comedy library, and laugh yourself back to health.

Affirm Yourself

If you're suffering from anxiety, you have to be your own best friend. Beef up your coping resources by constantly telling yourself that you're doing great. Acknowledge your innate talents and potentials. You may even shout, "You can do this!" every time you're faced with an anxiety-provoking situation. In moments of anxiety, there will be people who are interested only in bringing you down, but you don't have to be one of them. Lift yourself up!

When you experience symptoms of anxiety, the mind has a bias toward negativity. Even if there is evidence of positivity in a situation, an anxious person will often remain pessimistic and oppositional. That is why it's important to consciously think of ways in which the situation can be perceived as a positive. If you want to survive an anxiety attack, you need to develop some perspective. Everything may seem like an emergency at the height of anxiety, but over time things will look different. So remind yourself: "Today is not as bad as it seems. I will be laughing about all of this a week from now!"

So challenge yourself: what are some ways that the situation can be better? If you're about to take the SAT, for example, you can calm down by thinking of the best-case scenario—that you will pass with flying colors. If it's your turn to present in public speaking class, think of the situation as a way to showcase your savvy in debate. And even when things seem to be going poorly, think of other people who are in less fortunate situations, and appreciate what you have.

If you really want to get past your anxiety, you need to develop a sense of efficacy—that is, you need to have the knowledge that you are capable of surviving an anxiety attack. Have you survived a natural disaster? If yes, then congratulate yourself for being a resilient person. Were you once a wreck after a breakup but now you're fine? Then hold on to the certainty that you are capable of moving on. Recalling past successes is especially important at this point; they can give you a sense of your inner strength and give you a push to get back into tip-top condition. Every person has strengths—it's just a matter of letting those strengths out!

Say No to That Extra Cup of Coffee

Taking it easy on the coffee might seem like a simple tactic, but the effects can be drastic for some people. Caffeine is one of the most addictive drugs available, and you'd be surprised at how many people seem to run mainly on adrenaline and coffee. As mentioned earlier, caffeine can cause symptoms that simulate an anxiety attack and make anxiety feel a lot worse.

Say no to that extra cup—one cup of coffee should be enough, if you even need it at all. If you are a coffee addict, you'll be surprised at how much peace of mind a week of abstinence will bring. You'll breathe better, have reduced palpitations, and become less prone to nervousness. Positive things all around!

Write, Draw, Paint, Sing

It may be difficult to keep track of the many thoughts racing through your head when you're in the midst of an anxiety attack, but getting some of them out in a creative way can help alleviate some of the pressure. Writing down what you can catch may help you gain better awareness of what it is that's really making you anxious. Once you have your fears and apprehensions on paper, they can become easier to control and manage.

If a traumatic experience from your past continually haunts you, one thing you can do is vent through journaling. Called "testimonial therapy," this technique is recommended for people suffering from acute stress disorder and post-traumatic stress disorder. Writing an account of your traumatic experience over and over again is an excellent way to get your feelings out. For best results, make sure your latest account of the story magnifies your positive coping skills. Over time, your story should change from "an account of a victim" to an "account of a survivor."

Another effective way to leverage writing against your anxiety is to write a letter to yourself. Gestalt psychology argues that we have many versions of our self. Tap into the more proactive, brave, and competent you. Let him or her speak up, and write a letter to whip the anxious version of yourself into shape.

If writing isn't your style, try using another medium to get some of the anxious energy out. Draw or paint a picture, compose some music, or just sing your favorite song. Turning your anxiety into a physical piece of art is just another way to feel more in control when you feel overwhelmed.

Analyze Your Anxiety

Practitioners of neuro-linguistic programming (NLP) assert that the best way to battle an unwanted emotion is to fully accept and understand it. One aspect of emotion that you need to closely monitor is intensity.[15]

Ask yourself: on a scale of 1 to 10, with 10 being the most intense, how would I rate my current level of anxiety? Is today's anxiety less intense or more intense than the anxiety attack I had last week? Can I say that it is the most intense anxiety attack I've ever had? Understanding these details can leave you with a greater feeling of control over your anxiety reactions.

In addition to ranking the intensity of your attack, it is also very helpful to know what triggered it. If you want to get rid of your anxiety today, try reflecting on the question, why am I anxious? The more you understand the dynamics of your anxiety, the better off you'll be.

Exaggerate Your Predicament, or Don't

One way to manage fear is to come face-to-face with the worst-case scenario. After all, if you find you can survive the absolute worst, then every other anxiety trigger will seem small by comparison. So take the time to imagine the very worst thing that could happen to you, given your situation. Think about how you would get past the absolute worst-case scenario. If you know for certain that the worst is survivable, then you will be less prone to apprehension and worry.

On the opposite side of the same coin, you might try simply reminding yourself that everything is fine and that what you're feeling is just a part of life. At the height of anxiety, it may feel as if nothing is going right in the world. At times like these, it's important to remember that crises are part of everyday living and that conflict with others is unavoidable. Even if things are not going right in your universe, you're still experiencing normal everyday life. Thinking that life should be perfect all the time is one of the easiest ways to develop an anxiety disorder.

Get in Touch with Nature

Watching Mother Nature at work is a great way to calm oneself when in the middle of an anxiety attack. Go to a place where there are plenty of trees, and release to the universe all your pent-up emotions. Find an area where there is clean air and breathe deeply. Climbing something tall and looking at the vast expanses of space around you can make your troubles seem very, very small in comparison. You might even try playing with your favorite pet to ease the tension. For best results, reflect on the many metaphors offered by nature. The birth of a new plant from a dying seed can give you a lot of insight into how life should be. When the caterpillar says, "This is the end," the butterfly says, "This is the beginning."

Step Outside of Yourself, and Don't Go It Alone

Anxiety can make you self-centered—it can make you so focused on only what you are going through that you magnify every little thing that happens to you. This is why it wouldn't hurt to start practicing empathy every time you feel things are in extreme disarray. Think of a friend or a loved one who is also going through a difficult time, or find a cause or an advocacy you can adopt. When you're open to thinking about other people's concerns, you're ready to move on from your anxiety.

It's also important to remember that you don't have to own your anxiety by yourself. Tell your loved ones what you're going through—make them understand how anxiety feels. The more support you have during the difficult times, the more resilient you'll become. For best results, join fellow anxiety sufferers in a support group. Lone rangers are dead rangers, which is why if you want to survive anxiety, it helps to have others who can share the experience with you.

The belief that things can get better through one's efforts is a very important component of coping with anxiety. So make plans (with people!), and believe in those plans. Every little action that you do today can make a difference in how you feel tomorrow.

Let It Out

One of the main causes of anxiety is repressed anger. Sometimes you feel anxious because you are angry about a loss that you feel you don't deserve. At other times you may feel anxious because you're angry at the small amount of control you have over a situation. For that reason, it's important that you have handy ways of expressing your anger.

A simple but effective way of releasing repressed anger is by punching pillows. Spend a good ten minutes or so just expending the energy that seems to move in your hands. You may also try wringing towels for good effect. If punching pillows doesn't work, you might go for some scream therapy. Just go to a place where you won't be disturbed and where you won't disturb anyone, and scream at the top of your lungs. You may look silly for doing so, but it's a great source of release. You may even imagine all your worries are being released to the universe every time you open your mouth.

Serenity Rituals

Finally, it helps if you have a personal ritual that you can pull out anytime you find yourself becoming anxious and upset. These rituals can involve symbolic ways of warding off negativity, or figurative ways of letting go of one's burdens. Any of the previous suggestions might work for you, but here are a few different examples:

- Write down a source of your anxiety and then burn the paper. Let yourself feel the release of the anxiety, as if burning it out of your life.

- Feel all of your tension, clenching your hands tightly, as if putting all of that tension into your hands. Then take a deep breath and open your hands, letting the tension flow out of your body to be carried away on the winds. Shake your hands as if casting off all the bad energy.

- Wear a large plastic band on your wrist throughout the day. When you need to release the stress, stop, remove the band carefully from your wrist, and place it on the other wrist. This action will help focus your mind, and it will also help you find new goals for yourself. Count how many times in a day or a week you've needed to transfer the band, and see if you can lower that number. As the number gets smaller, so will the frequency of your panic attacks.

Everyone is different, and everyone responds to anxiety in different ways. Once you figure out what works for you to get your anxiety under control, you can begin to look more closely at what it is that happens in you during those attacks. Getting in tune with your thoughts and feelings is the next step in anxiety management.

Get in Tune with Your Thoughts and Feelings

If you're prone to experiencing anxiety, chances are your greatest enemy is your mind. When faced with a situation that has the potential to be anxiety-provoking, it's easy to imagine the worst or begin self-blame to the extent that the anxiety becomes magnified within seconds. If you really want to manage your anxiety, you have to be quick in catching your own self-destructive thoughts, as well as adept in transforming these negative thoughts into more facilitative ones.

THE POWER OF THOUGHTS

Stated simply, thoughts heavily influence what you feel. Take almost any event, and your perception of that event will color your thoughts and feelings. Imagine your spouse said that he was working late, but you spot him at a coffee shop with your best friend. These two things together might make you ask the question of whether or not they are having an affair. Now imagine that two days later, you're given a surprise party by your spouse and that same friend. It turns out the subterfuge was to keep the party a secret. Nothing about the fact that your husband told a fib and you saw him out with your friend has changed, but now your new knowledge of why changes how you feel about it.

It is important, then, for you to carefully monitor your thoughts so you can filter ideas that are anxiety-provoking and generally unhelpful to you. Since thoughts come automatically, this is often easier said than done. Sometimes you have already reacted to a thought even before you realize what it is. For instance, you may have lashed out at your spouse in anger before you even realized that you were coming up with jealous ideas. A lot of practice is needed if you want to be quick enough to catch the thoughts that trigger and exacerbate your anxiety.

COMMON ANXIETY-PROVOKING THOUGHTS

In the heat of the moment, you can come up with irrational thoughts without realizing it. Common anxiety-provoking thoughts fall into a few different categories.

Catastrophizing

A neologism that refers to the belief that something is far worse than it actually is, catastrophizing involves distortion of reality, because in most instances things are not as bad as they first seem. Catastrophizing can lead to panic, self-pity, and apprehension. It can also prevent one from seeing possible solutions because of the perception that one's situation is already a hopeless case. Consider the following example:

Jade was about to take a state board exam. However, on the eve of her test, she lost her review notes. Rationally, Jade knew that the loss shouldn't matter—she had already spent two months reviewing in preparation for the test. However, in her panic, she became convinced that losing her notes meant she wasn't going to remember any of the important information that would appear on the exam. She panicked to the extent that instead of relaxing her mind for the test, she spent the whole day trying to rewrite her notes from scratch.

From this example, you can see how catastrophizing can lead to useless worry and, consequently, useless action. The energy Jade spent on the missing notes could have been better spent relaxing her mind in time for the test.

"All or Nothing" Thinking

Another type of irrational thought that promotes anxiety is "all or nothing" thinking. When you have "all or nothing" thoughts, you rigidly subscribe to laws, rules, or circumstances, which in turn makes exceptions feel like failures. You may, for example, consciously or unconsciously subscribe to the belief that "everyone should like me." Or perhaps you think, "My work must be perfect all the time." The reality is that there will be moments when people hate you for no apparent reason (or what is more likely, not feel one way or another about you). There will also be times when your output is substandard despite hard work, just as it is likely to be superior from time to time. You have to be able to deal with those exceptions. You have to know that the "norm" is not going to happen every time, and that the "rules" put in place by "all or nothing" thinking are arbitrary. Rather than prevent anxiety, they do little other than contribute to it.

Disqualifying the Positive

In literature, there is a concept known as the "fallacy of the Romans"; it refers to a tendency to discount all the possible positive implications of an idea in favor of the negative implications. The term is exemplified by a famous line in the Monty Python film *Life of Brian*: "Apart from the sanitation, the medicine, education, wine, public order, irrigation, roads, a fresh water system, and public health, what have the Romans ever done for us?" If you persist in seeing the bad stuff, in spite of the litany of good stuff, then you are guilty of the fallacy of the Romans.

In many ways, people who are prone to anxiety tend to commit this fallacy. Life events become more threatening because we choose to give little value to positive interpretations of a situation, regardless of how clearly these positive interpretations may be presented. For example, you may persist in seeing a colleague's negative feedback as a reprimand, even if it's presented as good-natured advice. Or you may easily dismiss all the benefits of going outside and mingling with people, simply to justify your fear of going out in the world.

Educator and lecturer Leo Buscaglia made this observation about the seemingly innocuous word *but*. On Phil Donahue's talk show, Dr. Buscaglia made his point by saying, "Oh, Phil, you're so educated, and your show is wonderful, and your guests are terrific, your points are so well-made, you look great, BUT..."[18] With that one word, every compliment and positive thought has just been discounted into nothing. Eliminating the word *but* from your vocabulary can help fight this tendency to disqualify the positive.

Negative Self-Labels

Another habit that can cause or aggravate the symptoms of anxiety is called "negative self-labeling." As the term implies, negative self-labeling refers to the habit of tagging, oneself with self-defeating adjectives. For instance, saying, "Ugh, I am so stupid!" is an example of negative self-labeling, as is saying, "I am the ugliest person in the world."

Although self-labeling seems like a harmless habit at first, it can do a lot of damage in the long run, because what we call ourselves tends to represent our self-esteem. As mentioned previously, low self-esteem is one of the major causes of anxiety. The more negatively you view yourself, the more prone to anxiety you become.

Note also that criticizing things or circumstances that you are in can also be considered self-labeling. "This is the worst job in the world!" So if you chose it, does that mean you are bad, too? "This house has so much wrong with it!" Are you also saying that you made a poor choice, or that you are at fault for not doing more? Even if your negativity doesn't have "I" or "me" in it, it can still imply something negative about yourself.

HOW TO DEAL WITH UNHELPFUL THOUGHTS

A school of psychotherapy called cognitive behavioral therapy (CBT) states that if you want to manage negative thoughts, you have to consciously exert an effort to arrest these negative thoughts and replace them with positive ones. To do this, you have to employ the 3C strategy: cease, calm, change.[17]

Step 1: Cease

The first step in managing unhelpful thoughts is to actively, consciously stop thinking these negative thoughts. The best way to stop focusing on this set of bad thoughts is simply to distract yourself.

This may seem counterintuitive; after all, wouldn't controlling the runaway thoughts be better than not thinking about them at all? The key word in that question is *runaway*. If an old-fashioned wooden cart is rolling down a hill toward you, it's not likely that you'll stop it by standing in front of it; it will mow you down and keep going, and you'll be worse for wear.

For a more practical example, try not to think of a pink elephant. For those with anxiety disorders, that elephant will push harder and harder into the mind until it's literally all that can be thought of! To stop thinking of the pink elephant, divert your attention elsewhere—a yellow giraffe, an orange tiger, or a polka-dotted lion. Distraction will derail the power of that overwhelming thought and give you a chance to regain your mental control.

How do you distract yourself? A recognized (if a bit painful) technique is to snap a rubber band against one's wrist whenever an unhelpful thought is occurs; the sharp shock diverts one's attention quite effectively. Another method is to do something physical—jump up and down, break into song, snap your fingers in a complicated rhythm, or "play the bongos" on a desk or a tabletop. You might also try shifting your focus to a strange or comical image. Fans of *The Carol Burnett Show* might recall her send-up called "Went with the Wind," in which she (as Scarlett O'Hara) comes downstairs in a dress made from window curtains—with the curtain rod visible across her shoulders.

Step 2: Calm

Breaking free of the frantic emotional cycle, your thoughts become your own; at this point, the thoughts you want are calming ones. In the previous chapter, you found a number of techniques to calm yourself and begin to think more clearly. Basic stress-management skills include breathing exercises, listening to calming music, visualizing being in a peaceful place, and even aromatherapy—the use of certain familiar, favorite, or calming scents. If you are of a religious nature, you may find that prayer or meditation helps. Let yourself surrender your worries and frustration, trusting that you will be guided and given strength.

Step 3: Change

The last step is to deliberately transform negative thoughts into positive ones. This process is called *reframing*: changing perspective on a situation so that you can see another angle you haven't thought about before. For example, if thinking that you might lose your job over a small mistake gives you anxiety, think instead about all the possible reasons your employer would want to keep you. If you think that you're a failure in life, think of how you have learned from your mistakes, particularly the times when that learning has led to a success in your life. Perhaps you can't please everyone all the time—can you really think of someone who can?

Consider this example of employing the 3C strategy:

David suffers from obsessive-compulsive disorder. Despite his better judgment, he spends every minute of the day cleaning his home. He can't help himself—he feels anxious if he doesn't scrub his walls at least twice a day, or if he doesn't sweep his floor at least five times. One of his pet peeves is seeing footprints on his carpet, which is why he diligently straightens and smoothes his carpet every time there's a mark.

One night, David invited friends over for dinner. Naturally, the rooms became messy—the carpet was filled with shoe prints, there were dirty dishes all over the place, and the furniture he had meticulously arranged was in disarray. Seeing the mess, David felt a panic attack coming on—he felt as if he had to get everything organized immediately. Feeling the compulsion to clean coming over him, he *ceased*—by loudly singing his favorite song in an attempt to think of something else. Between verses and choruses, he *calmed* himself by performing deep-breathing exercises (which, he realized, gave him more air to sing with, and the improvement in his singing further distracted him from the anxiety).

Once he had calmed his thoughts, David tried to come up with new perspectives to *change* his way of thinking about the situation. There was mess, yes, but this mess was a sign that he had a lot of friends. Having a mess-free home meant no loved ones ever came to visit and that he would be all alone. A little mess now that he could take care of calmly after the fact was a small price for having a wonderful evening with friends.

WHAT ARE FEELINGS?

So far, this chapter has talked about thoughts and how they can increase the anxiety that you feel. But people are not computers, nor are people simply the sum of their thoughts. Feelings, too, play a great role in the degree to which people experience anxiety, and getting in touch with your feelings is at least as important as getting a handle on your thoughts.

Feelings refer to subjective experiences of emotions—things like anger, happiness, sadness, fondness, and joy. There are even more subjective notions, such as "feeling trapped" or "feeling lost." It's difficult to define what a feeling is, and perhaps for that reason, many people seem to ignore their feelings (or at least fail to describe or report them) in favor of thoughts or other more objective observations. For instance, if you ask a group of people, "How do you feel?" you'll often get nonfeeling replies like, "Everything is going fine," or "I think I am going to be all right." There is a pronounced tendency to ignore or discount feelings.

Many factors contribute to this phenomenon. Childhood experience counts for a lot. If you are male and were raised to think that "big boys don't cry," you may find that your adult experiences of sadness or loss are particularly uncomfortable. If you were taught that expressing anger or disapproval in any way, no matter how mild, is inappropriate, you may never have learned how to assert your personal preferences or express your anger appropriately. If at any age you experienced ridicule for expressing an emotion, there is a strong likelihood that you would resist sharing your emotions with anyone in the future.

Feelings Are Neither Right nor Wrong

Feelings are amoral—they are neither right nor wrong. They also come without warning; you don't choose to get upset, you simply become upset. You can't be blamed for what you feel—for something you don't rationally control. The only thing that can be judged is *how you react to those feelings.* It's not what you feel but what you do about it that makes the difference. You can feel outrage over an incident, but expressing that outrage with violence is not appropriate in most situations. Actions made "in the heat of the moment" are often not the best courses of action. Author Robert Heinlein's famous character Lazarus Long advises against taking rash action: "[Killing someone] is only a temporary pleasure, and it's bound to get you talked about."[18]

As we've said time and again, anxiety often overcomes rational thinking. For that reason, it's not good to follow any rash course of action when in the throes of an anxiety attack. What's even more important to remember is that you're allowed to feel anything. You're no more "wrong" to feel anxious than to feel angry, sad, or happy. This knowledge may help prevent you from blaming yourself for the anxiety. The stormy emotion is unpleasant, but letting it flow through you and waiting it out is often the best way to get rid of it. Repressing or denying a feeling frequently makes it worse. Let the emotion be what it is, and experience what Scottish psychiatrist R. D. Laing called "diving through [the emotional turmoil] and coming out the other side"—an exercise he felt would make you stronger for having experienced it.[19]

How Do You Know What You're Feeling?

One good way to know what you're feeling is a technique called "journaling"—that is, you create a diary of all the emotions that you are going through. Journaling is an excellent way of venting—releasing your feelings to the outer world so that they don't bother you as much. Simply write out exactly what you feel, without editing for grammar or style. The more authentic you are when you create your journal, the more effective the process will be for you.

To get the most out of your journal, periodically read back over what you've written. The journal may help you uncover patterns, see connections between stimuli and emotions, and provide insights into how much control you have gained over your panic attacks. Reading how you overcame previous attacks, you may realize in the grip of a new attack, "This will not look nearly as bad in thirty or forty-five minutes; I don't have to give in to these paicked feelings."

Another way to get in touch with your feelings is to find someone—a friend or a professional counselor—who can listen to what you're going through with empathy. Empathy refers to the skill of being able to put oneself in another person's shoes. Someone who is empathizing with you is trying to understand how you feel. Having someone empathize with you can make you feel less alone, which in turn can give you strength to face the object of your anxiety.

Finally, you may want to create some "freaking-out" time in your schedule—time when you're free to give in to your anxiety. For example, you can give yourself exactly one hour to scream, cry, pull your hair, or throw a tantrum—just so you can release your emotions. It's always better to give emotions a moment when they have free rein rather than to repress them. Repressing emotions doesn't mean they will go away—they'll just find more passive-aggressive ways of expressing themselves.

Although these are great ways to get in touch with your feelings, creating an anxiety log over time can really help you get to the root of what causes your symptoms.

WHAT IS AN ANXIETY LOG?

An anxiety log is essentially a detailed diary of moments when you experience anxiety. In a shorthand fashion, you note six factors:

1. **DATE** and time I felt anxious

2. How I know I was anxious **(SYMPTOMS)**

3. What I was **THINKING** at the time

4. What I was **FEELING** at the time

5. What I was **DOING** at the time

6. The **EFFECT** of the anxiety on me

When making your log, you can abbreviate each of the factors to make it more efficient, as shown in the following sample. Writing line by line rather than in a grid is recommended—give yourself plenty of room to make notes and include as much or as little detail as you feel is useful. Remember, the better sense you have of what leads to anxiety attacks, the better you will be able to manage them in the future.

1. **DATE:** Saturday, November 6

2. **SYMPTOMS:** Hands clammy, sweaty; heavy feeling in my chest

3. **THINKING:** The bills are not going to get paid on time.

4. **FEELING:** Overwhelmed, too much responsibility, too much to do and take care of

5. **DOING:** Reading bank's notice of payment due

6. **EFFECT:** Can't concentrate on my work; mind wandering with "what if" scenarios

If you're more used to using a keyboard than writing by hand, there's nothing wrong with typing up a document with this information. However, since you're probably not always at your keyboard, carrying a small notebook with you will encourage you to write short notes when the anxious feelings actually occur. If you wish, you can transfer the information to a computer document later. This might also give you a chance to reflect further on the incident, bringing up new observations or information that will add even more depth to your log.

An anxiety log can help surface the unique dynamics of your anxious feelings. One of the best ways you can manage anxiety is to demystify it—understand when the anxiety comes, how it comes, why it comes, and the impact it has upon you. When you understand the routine of it all, you can better anticipate attacks and make more adequate preparations. You can also better recognize your unique triggers and symptoms of anxiety, since anxiety affects people differently.

It's best if you can write down a description of each anxiety attack as soon as it happens. However, as you may already have considered, you might feel too overwhelmed to make notes as the attack is happening. If that happens, don't let your inability to write details make your anxiety worse; give yourself permission to write it down later.

The best value of this log is that it will help you look for patterns—certain dynamics that recur over time. For example, does your anxiety come only at particular times of the day? Some people experience anxiety mostly in the morning hours, while others experience anxiety primarily during weekends. If the first of each month carries certain responsibilities with it (rent, reports for work, etc.), you may find more anxiety attacks occurring on or around that date. Knowing the dates and times that your attacks occurred can help you anticipate when the next one might happen, and allow you to better understand the factors that induce anxiety in you.

You can also check whether your anxiety is triggered by particular thoughts, feelings, or behaviors. If, for example, you have three entries of anxiety attacks caused by thinking about bills and payables, then you know that financial obligations rank high on your list of anxiety triggers. Knowing what causes your anxiety can help you better understand how to prevent or lessen the effects of similar attacks, and can give you some direction as far as processing your feelings. For best results, identify your top three triggers of anxiety by monitoring and comparing the similarities among attacks over a period of about a month.

If you have time, don't just create an anxiety log—create a "no anxiety" log as well. This is a record of all the times you felt calm, relaxed, and free from worries. If you can figure out what triggers tranquility in your person, you can better find ways to manage your anxiety. This suggestion may sound like a variation of "stop and smell the roses," but taking that brief time out of your day is actually very good advice—unless, of course, you're allergic to roses.

Now that you have looked at ways to better understand your own thoughts, feelings, and triggers in the relatively short term, it's time to learn the next step in anxiety management: developing behavioral techniques and mental strategies for dealing with objects of anxiety.

Develop Behavioral Techniques and Mental Strategies

If there's one behavior that characterizes anxiety, it's avoidance. You won't be able to help it—naturally you will want to avoid the object of your anxiety as much as possible. If you have social anxiety disorder, for example, you will go out of your way to avoid being in social situations or situations that would expose your perceived weaknesses to other people. If you have arachnophobia, or fear of spiders, you will not want to go to the section of the zoo where the spiders are, and you might not even dare to venture into your own basement. As much as possible, you will naturally steer clear of whatever triggers a negative reaction in you.

This is no problem if the object of your anxiety can be easily avoided without causing any significant impact on your life. You can easily manage a fear of giraffes, for example, because there is little likelihood you will encounter a giraffe in an average neighborhood. But what if you're afraid of heights? So many offices are located on higher floors of buildings, and you can't say you won't show up at a job interview just because it's on the nineteenth floor. Some objects of anxiety you will have to face head on.

This is where behavioral techniques to manage anxiety come in—specifically, the technique of *desensitization*. As the name suggests, desensitization is the process of becoming less sensitive to a stimulus by gradually exposing oneself to that stimulus—in this case, the object of anxiety—until one develops a growing comfort in its presence. Desensitization also means learning to gradually cope with anxiety until one is ready to stop avoiding the objects and scenarios that cause it.

STEPS TO EFFECTIVE DESENSITIZATION

There are three steps to effective desensitization: (1) creating a ladder of escalating exposure to the object of your anxiety, (2) adding relaxation techniques to gradual exposure, and (3) rewarding yourself with each step up the ladder to reinforce the effects.

Create a Ladder of Escalating Exposure to the Object of Your Anxiety

If you want to eventually get used to the object of your anxiety, you have to be exposed to it in gradually increasing degrees. If you're afraid of snakes, for example, perhaps it wouldn't hurt to begin the desensitization process by being first exposed to pictures of snakes. Once the pictures of snakes no longer trigger anxiety in you, then you can start holding 3-D models of snakes made from clay. When you're used to the model, you can touch the skin shed by a snake. Then you can begin to look at a live snake from afar. When this no longer triggers anxious feelings in you, you can start standing a short distance from a live snake. And when you're finally ready, you can start touching a nonpoisonous snake with your hands. The key is to not shock your system—likely triggering anxiety—but to allow yourself time to get used to what your systems considers a scary prospect.

Here's another example: If you want to rid yourself of the fear of public speaking, perhaps you can start by getting used to how it feels to stand behind a podium in an empty auditorium. When this no longer triggers anxiety in you, you can deliver a speech to the empty room. Once you've successfully delivered your speech, start letting people in—one or two people to start, and then a small crowd. And when you're finally ready, the highest rung of your escalation ladder can be giving a speech to a roomful of people.

Add Relaxation Techniques to Gradual Exposure

Once you have defined the components of the ladder, it's time to plan how to manage your gradual exposure. To avoid "freaking out" every time you step up the ladder, you need to associate your anxiety-provoking situation with something relaxing—even gratifying. For this reason, you add relaxation techniques every time you are exposed to the object of your anxiety.

Let's use again the example of the fear of public speaking. In that example, the first step of the ladder is simply to stand behind a podium or lectern in an otherwise empty auditorium. Before walking up to stand at the lectern, use some of the relaxation techniques discussed earlier. Backstage or in the wings, sit in a chair and practice deep-breathing exercises, or imagine yourself to be in a happy place. When you feel calm, you can then walk up to the lectern and stand behind it. As you stand there, continue to breathe deeply, maintaining the calm as best you can. If it begins to feel stressful, walk slowly away from the lectern and back into the wings. If you wish, you can try regaining your calm and returning to the podium, or congratulate yourself on your first steps and call it a day.

The object is to become calm and remain that way as you walk to and stand behind the lectern—that's the first step. When you can do that, you can try the next step, which is reading part or all of your speech to the empty auditorium. As before, if you begin to feel anxious, step away and regain your calm. At each step, you'll find that you can "climb the ladder" higher and higher—do more and more—while still remaining calm. Eventually, you'll be able to deliver your speech calmly, or at the very least without debilitating anxiety.

Reward Yourself Every Time You Step up the Ladder

Although being gradually exposed to an object of anxiety looks easy on paper, in reality it can be a difficult process—one that takes a lot of time and willpower. You may, for example, find yourself panicking at just the first rung of your exposure ladder. That is okay; in fact, it's common. You can climb the ladder with a combination of persistence and reward.

Prepare rewards for each step of the ladder, and if possible, make each reward bigger with each successive step. Perhaps you've set your heart on a new electronic gizmo; give yourself a financial reward for each step, building up to the full price by the time you get to the end: ten dollars for the first step, twenty for the next, forty for the next, and so on. Divide the total cost in this fashion until you can purchase your new gizmo when you have accomplished your final goal. (Don't forget to add sales tax.)

Even simple rewards like ice cream or tickets to a movie can be motivating, if you really want them. Keep rewarding yourself for each step, because you deserve it—you're accomplishing great things, one step at a time.

GOING SOLUTION-FOCUSED

Anxiety can trap you in limbo by making you feel that the problem is too big for you to control. If you're panicking because of a looming deadline, for example, anxiety can make you feel that no matter what you do, you won't ever finish on time. If you are anxious because of the stack of credit card bills you receive every month, anxiety can make you feel as if working 24/7 isn't ever going to create a dent in the payables. The result: you get stuck wanting to do more but feeling that even if you do, it's no use.

The reality is, no matter how big the problem, there is always something you can do at the current moment to make it smaller or more manageable—even if only by a tiny bit. The deadline may be near, for example, and there might be no way you can hit it, but you can negotiate for a new due date. You don't know if your employer might be open to the new schedule, but at least you actively tried to find a way out of your predicament. Similarly, your bills may cumulatively be too high for you to pay off in a month, but you can pay off the one with the highest rate of interest. This way you are sure you have fewer penalties to think about. A portion of the problem is solved, and you take an active role in solving it.

This kind of attitude is what is called being "solution-focused." Every time you feel debilitating anxiety, the first thing you do is challenge yourself: *What can I do right now to make it better?* Your immediate solution may not solve the entire problem, but it can create progress. As a result, you won't feel as helpless as before. As many self-help practitioners will assert, you must always focus on the solution, not on the problem.

What makes this attitude particularly effective in managing anxiety is that small changes can lead to big changes. Once you have an example of how even small efforts can influence the outcome of the situation, you will want to do still more. Just as the ladder of escalating exposure from the last section helps you take on a new situation one step at a time, so does the act of making small changes embolden you to make still more, larger changes. Self-confidence is a powerful tool against anxiety.

Consider the following ways to seek solutions:

Look for Exceptions

One way to see what will work is to look for exceptions to the rule. Let's say that meeting new people brings on anxiety for you. Look through your past and ask, "Has there ever been a time when I introduced myself to someone new and it felt okay (or at least didn't panic me so badly)?" If you can find one, this is the exception to the rule that you're searching for. What was different during that encounter? For this example, let's say that you were okay introducing yourself to someone new when you were in the company of a friend—the stability of someone you already knew. That's your solution: have a friend with you to help overcome your fear of meeting new people. As you have more successful encounters with meeting new people, you may find that you can do so on your own—the exception will become the rule.

Ask the Miracle Question

If your current situation feels terrible—let's say you get anxious when you're left alone in your house—what would be different if you miraculously didn't feel anxious in that situation anymore? This is the miracle question: "If a miracle should happen, and all your problems somehow were solved, what would be different?" You would be able to do things on your own that you can't do now, and you might enjoy solitary activities. Notice also how you feel in that new scenario—what emotional changes have occurred? By looking into this miracle future, you can begin to find rewards in a situation that until then seemed to be filled with only anxiety.

A different version of the miracle question is the crystal ball question. You can ask yourself: "If you can peek into a crystal ball that shows a future where all is well, what would be different?" Again, look for the positive feelings and the rewarding activities that will be available to you. This vision of a better time may provide clues to solutions that can get you there.

Identify What Part of the Problem You Can Control

Sometimes there is a reason to be overwhelmed by the problem that you're facing—everything about it is beyond control. If you are experiencing post-traumatic stress over surviving a natural disaster, for example, and the effects of the disaster are still ongoing, there is little you can do but wait it out. What you can do is focus on what aspects of the problem you can control. You may not be able to control weather conditions, but you can control how you spend your day while waiting out the storm. When you acknowledge that you still are capable of changing some aspect of your situation, you can better manage your anxiety.

Overcoming Anxiety

STEP **6**

Make Healthful, Long-Term Lifestyle Changes

STEP **7**

Learn to Deal with Anxiety-Inducing People and Situations

....

The previous two sections talked about the importance of understanding what anxiety is and where it comes from. It also looked at specific tactics you can take to combat anxiety in the moment and in the short term—everything from specific breathing exercises to getting in touch with your thoughts and feelings to developing mental techniques. These next few final steps look at lifestyle changes as well as ways to cope with anxiety-inducing people and situations that can really help you ultimately overcome your anxiety in the long run.

Make Healthful, Long-Term Lifestyle Changes

Changing one's diet may seem like an odd way of treating mental health conditions, but scientists long ago discovered a relationship between food and mood. In particular, there are foods and drinks known to trigger and aggravate anxiety episodes. There are also foods and drinks that are known to have a calming effect on the nervous system. If you have an anxiety condition, the old adage "you are what you eat" may be more true than you think!

WHAT TO AVOID

For starters, let's take a look at what you should eliminate from your diet if you want to be able to manage your anxiety better. This advice is important, because many of the foods that we classify as "comfort foods" may actually do more harm than good.

Stimulants

Stimulants in general are not advisable if you are suffering from anxiety episodes. Stimulants increase the work of the nervous system, which in turn leads to anxiety-like symptoms such as shortness of breath, palpitations, and gastrointestinal problems. The more stimulants you take in a day, the greater your chances of experiencing an attack.

Caffeine. As mentioned earlier, one stimulant that you should really avoid is caffeine, which can be found in coffee, tea, and some sodas. Aside from provoking an adrenal response in the body, this stimulant depletes the body of the chemicals it needs to regulate mood and affect. The recommended dose of caffeine is just 50 mg a day, and less is better. To put this in perspective: The ordinary cup of coffee (8 oz) has about 95 mg of caffeine; espresso is highly concentrated and can have as much as 45 mg of caffeine *per ounce*. Coca-Cola is said falsely to be "worse" (more caffeinated) than coffee, but it has only 34 mg per 12 oz can. "Energy drinks" contain anything from slightly more caffeine than coffee (Full Throttle has about 100 mg per 8 oz) to truly terrifying amounts (Redline Power Rush contains 350 mg of caffeine per 2.5 oz).[20]

Nicotine. As strong a stimulant as caffeine, nicotine promotes physiological arousal and vasoconstriction, and it induces your heart to work harder than it should. The apparent use of smoking a cigarette to "calm down" is much more closely related to satisfying the craving for nicotine than it is to any physiological tranquility; one becomes "calm" by satisfying the need for more nicotine. In this way, smoking resembles an obsessive-compulsive cycle. Studies show that cigarette smoking increases the risk of developing a panic disorder.

Stimulant-type drugs. Last, it helps to remove stimulant-type drugs from your system—unless they are absolutely necessary to your health. Prescription stimulants and recreational stimulants—such as amphetamines and cocaine, respectively—increase the risk of generalized anxiety disorder among those who take them.

Salt

Salt depletes the body of potassium, which is critical for the nervous system to function properly. It can also cause elevated blood pressure and heart problems. If you're prone to anxiety, it's best that you avoid foods that have a high sodium content. This includes some pretzels and fried potatoes, cheese, potato salad, sliced meats, and stews. Salt is also a staple in most fast-food products.

To be safe, try to limit your intake of salt. The National Institutes of Health suggests that healthy adults should have no more than 2,300 mg of salt per day—about one teaspoon.[21] Nutritional information on packaged foods will help you keep an eye on your intake. As a rule of thumb, 1 oz of salted pretzels contains about 360 mg of salt. Watch for "hidden sources" of salt in your cooking, such as salted butter (only 2 mg per tablespoon, but it adds up) and sauces (soy sauce on your egg roll will cost you over 500 mg per tablespoon).

Alcohol

Alcohol is a natural depressant. Although it can make you feel calm and sedate in the short term, it can also be dehydrating. That's the reason why drinking too much results in a hangover—a hangover is your brain's reaction to losing water, so if you don't keep your-self hydrated when you drink, you get a nasty headache a few hours later. The dehydration caused by alcohol consumption can often exacerbate anxiety for those who are already prone to having anxiety or panic attacks. The accompanying depression contributes to their feeling of helplessness, resulting in more feel-ings of frustration.

Hormones in Meat

Most meat products sold commercially come from livestock that are fed with growth hormones. One hormone in particular—diethylstilbestrol (DES)—is known to increase agitation and restlessness. It may even be responsible for the development of breast tumors and cancers. As much as possible, choose organically raised meat in your diet.

Sweets

Cakes, ice cream, and all other sugary treats lead the list of things we should stay away from when we're anxious or depressed. Since they taste good, we gravitate to sugary foods first to make us feel better, and the accompanying sugar rush gives us a temporary high. Unfortunately, it is also the same sugar rush that will cause your body to crash and burn a few hours later. This is especially true if you have any sugar-related issues like hypoglycemia or diabetes.

Most people who indulge their sweet tooth at work usually feel listless and fatigued during the middle of the day, making it more difficult for them to focus on everyday tasks. This, in turn, leads to poor performance and low job satisfaction, ultimately resulting in frustration and irritation. Those who indulge late in the evening—right before bed—may find that they have difficulty sleeping. The sugar rush stays on long after you're ready to go to bed, potentially robbing you of a few hours of rest.

WHAT TO EAT

Some readers may feel that eating anything could be an issue! Not so—here are some "good guy" foods that can actually help you overcome your anxiety.

Omega-3-Rich Foods

Foods rich in omega-3 fatty acids—salmon, tuna, sardines, and tofu, for example—help lower blood cholesterol and attack the buildup of plaque in the bloodstream, thus improving circulation. The protein in these foods breaks down slowly in the bloodstream, which helps stabilize sugar levels in the body. This, in turn, helps alleviate feelings of tension and anxiety that may be caused by too much or too little sugar in the blood.

Dark Chocolate

Eating dark chocolate in moderation helps increase levels of the feel-good chemicals serotonin, dopamine, and norepinephrine in the body. This means that dark chocolate can help induce feelings of calm and relaxation. Further, dark chocolate has less processed sugar (generally speaking) than other sweets; thus it goes into the bloodstream slowly rather than causing the blood sugar level to spike. Note, though, that dark chocolate has high amounts of saturated fat and should be consumed sparingly.

Berries

If you need a snack that will not leave you feeling guilty, consider munching on berries. Berries are rich in vitamin C, which helps fight the stress hormone cortisol—which in turn can alleviate anxiety. The complex carbohydrates in berries are also slow to turn into sugar, which means you won't have to fight the hyperactivity that comes with a sugar rush. One caution: if you are prone to generating more stomach acid during periods of stress (the source of stress-related ulcers in the stomach), the acidity of berries could cause more harm than good. Enjoy them in moderation.

Oranges

Like berries, oranges are also rich in vitamin C, which helps fight stress. Research shows that people who take 1,000 mg of vitamin C before giving a speech have lower cortisol or stress hormone levels than those who don't get their dose of vitamin C. Eating the orange itself, rather than drinking orange juice, provides fiber (in the form of pulp) and helps slow the absorption of sugar into the system. Drinking orange juice provides a faster influx of sugar than does eating an orange, and because of the ascorbic acid (vitamin C) present in oranges, the same caution cited for berries (regarding stomach issues) applies.

Tryptophan-Rich Foods

The neurotransmitter serotonin—the neurotransmitter responsible for calm and relaxation—is produced from the amino acid tryptophan, and it can pay to add foods rich in tryptophan to your diet. These foods include milk, cheese, yogurt, bananas, peanut butter, and oats. Tryptophan is also found in turkey, which may be another reason people often feel sleepy after a big Thanksgiving dinner. (It's also valuable to remember this if you're planning to have a turkey sandwich for lunch at work.)

Folic-Acid-Rich Foods

A deficiency of folic acid in the body has been known to contribute to anxiety as well as mood disorders such as depression. It's important to eat foods rich in folic acid to maintain a balance of the chemical in one's system. Such food includes spinach, barley, lentils, brown rice, dates, fish, and oranges. The recommended dose of folic acid, according to the National Institutes of Health, is 200–500 mcg (micrograms, or 1/1,000 of a gram) per day. Half a cup of boiled spinach contains approximately 131 mcg; a cup of medium-grain white rice provides about 90 mcg.

AND DON'T FORGET YOUR EATING HABITS!

Finally, it pays to remember that managing anxiety lies not just in what you eat but also in how you eat it. Some prime examples:

- Take your time when eating; don't fight the clock. If you find yourself rushing, try putting your fork or spoon down.

- Don't skip meals. The irregularity in your blood sugar levels will come back to haunt you.

- Never eat while driving. Apart from feeling rushed to pack in the food, you more than double your "distraction factor," increasing your risk of having an accident—a sure source of yet more stress.

- When possible, eat when you're hungry, not when the clock says that it's time to eat. This allows your body to find its natural pattern, which not only lowers stress but also allows your body to function more efficiently.

- If you have blood sugar issues, you may want to try a trick that diabetics call "grazing." Rather than trying to get your nutrition in three large meals per day, break it up into four to six smaller meals, eaten at intervals during the day. The many advantages gained from this technique include better control of calories, carbs, and portions; less chance of over-fullness and becoming tired from needing to digest a large meal (the tiredness is called "postprandial narcosis"); and more energy from having "fuel" provided regularly when it is needed.

EXERCISE THERAPY

If you're suffering from anxiety, one of the last things you probably want to do is exercise. After all, it is often much more tempting to stay cooped up alone in one's room, nursing feelings of apprehension, than it is to get out in the world and sweat. However, exercise is one of the most effective ways of managing anxiety. It may not be able to cure anxiety disorders completely, but it can help alleviate the symptoms significantly.

Exercise and the Brain

We've all heard of the runner's high or the surfer's high; that is, people who engage in physical sports often feel as if they're in a peak mental state after their efforts. The reason for that is simple: exercise helps stabilize the amount of "happy" chemicals like serotonin and dopamine in the body, helping improve general mood. It almost works like a natural antidepressant.

Even more so, it helps renew the mind. Researchers from Princeton University found that exercise helps stimulate the creation of new brain cells—brain cells that are resistant to stress.[22] Therefore, the more you exercise, the greater number of these "stress-resistant" brain cells you will have, leaving you more relaxed and calm even when faced with anxiety-provoking situations. You can almost say that exercise renews the hardware of your brain so that you always function in optimum condition.

Exercise and Meditation

Generally, Westerners think of Eastern meditation techniques as sitting in a certain position and trying to think about nothing at all—hardly a description of a kind of exercise, right? In truth, however, several forms of Eastern meditation include multiple body positions (yoga) and even "moving meditations," such as tai chi and qigong. In these disciplines, the careful focus of the body as it goes through the movement of the exercise stimulates muscles and calms the mind.

SIMPLE EXERCISES TO DO

The cost of gym memberships has been rising steadily for many years as more people discover the advantage of going to a particular place to perform regular exercises. Because of our ever-changing schedules and increasing obligations, it can be difficult to set a specific time to do these things. "Making time for yourself" is also an important aspect of healing your stress and anxiety; if that seems all but impossible to do, don't "stress out" about that on top of everything else. Here are some ways to incorporate more physical activity into your daily routine.

One word of caution: our society has become increasingly sedentary over the years, as more and more tasks are performed at desks rather than in fields or factories. Begin any exercise or set of exercises slowly; if you get too tired or start feeling sore, stop for the day. Give yourself leeway to start with as few as three or four sit-ups, toe touches, or other exercise. Add one more every other day; then give yourself leave to stop at, say, ten each day for as much as a week. When that seems like no work at all, add some more. To use a runner's terms, this is not a sprint, it's a marathon—slow, steady pacing will get you to where you want to be.

Walking and Cycling

If your home is near your workplace, opt to walk or ride a bike rather than drive a car or take a bus or a train. Walking, along with jogging, is considered the most popular and detoxifying exercise. A daily fifteen-minute walk can result in significant health improvement. Remember that it is better to walk outside in fresh air, so opt for outdoor exercise rather than indoor as often as you can.

Simple Stretches

Whereas walking and cycling are *aerobic* exercises—helping your heart and lungs—stretching exercises focus on muscles to strengthen, relax, and tone them. Whenever you can, take a minute to stand up at your desk and stretch your body. Wegman's, a grocery store chain in New York State, actually announces "micro-stretch" breaks for employees and shoppers. The technique has paid off in fewer physical stress injuries on the job.[23]

Some simple stretching exercises that you can do at work or at home include stretching your arms high in the air as far as you can reach and then gradually setting them back down, bending down and reaching for your toes with your knees straight, and squatting in your seat and standing up repeatedly.

Standing Up

Yes, standing up! Research reveals that you actually burn more calories standing up than sitting down. Thus, it helps to find ways to stand up as much as you can. If you work in an office, try standing up to take your phone calls; you might even find that your voice is stronger and more authoritative when standing than it is when you are sitting. If you can walk around your office while you're on the phone, you may discover that the movement helps you think, as well as stretch your muscles.

PRESCRIPTION MEDICATION

If even after making changes to your diet and lifestyle, you still find anxiety really difficult to manage, you might want to consider talking to your physician or mental health professional about a prescription for anti-anxiety medications. These drugs can help restore the balance of brain chemicals, or neurotransmitters, occurring with anxiety and make you feel calmer and more relaxed.

You can get a prescription for anti-anxiety medications only after a consultation with a licensed psychiatrist or general practitioner—your doctor will decide if medication is your best option. For best results, don't rely on anxiety medication alone, but mix medication with psychotherapy and other self-help techniques to manage anxiety. Considering that anti-anxiety medications have significant side effects, it's also advisable to exhaust nonpharmaceutical ways of dealing with anxiety before considering medication.

There are many kinds of prescription anti-anxiety medications. Among them are benzodiazepines, antidepressants, and beta-blockers.

Benzodiazepines

Benzodiazepines—also called "minor tranquilizers"—are drugs that reduce anxiety by depressing the central nervous system. They are currently one of the most prescribed categories of drugs in the world. Popular benzodiazepines include alprazolam (Xanax), diazepam (Valium), lorazepam (Ativan), prazepam (Centrax), clorazepate (Tranxene), and oxazepam (Serax). Benzodiazepines were introduced about thirty years ago as an alternative to barbiturates—which have many side effects—for treating anxiety.

The main advantage of benzodiazepines is their quick efficacy—you can feel relief from anxiety within ten to fifteen minutes of taking the drug. This makes it convenient, and relief can be made available on an as-needed basis. However, the effects of these drugs generally last for only the short term, which means you have to retake the drug if you want long-term efficacy.

Like most medications, benzodiazepines have many side effects, including drowsiness, poor concentration, motor incoordination, slow reaction time, and memory impairment. They may also promote what is called "paradoxical disinhibition" in some patients—that is, they promote the symptoms they are supposed to cure. Researchers are still unsure what specific factors promote a positive response to benzodiazepines and what factors cause paradoxical disinhibition. Benzodiazepines are also known to cause physical and psychological dependency. This medicine is not recommended for people with a history of drug abuse. If you take benzodiazepines with any regularity, you will have to be gradually weaned off them to manage withdrawal symptoms. Consult your doctor before discontinuing the use of these drugs.

Antidepressants

As the name implies, antidepressants are drugs used to treat depression. However, they can also be prescribed for people with anxiety disorders. Antidepressants are most commonly given to people who are suffering from panic attacks, agoraphobia, or both.

There are many types of antidepressants. They include:

Selective serotonin reuptake inhibitors (SSRI). These drugs increase the levels of the neurotransmitter serotonin in the brain by inhibiting its absorption by nerve cells. Serotonin is important for a person's subjective feeling of calm and relaxation, and serves as a messenger chemical of the central nervous system. Popular brands of SSRIs include Prozac, Zoloft, Paxil, Celexa, and Lexapro.

SSRIs have side effects, although they are often considered mild compared with the side effects of benzodiazepines and other types of antidepressants. Potential side effects of SSRIs include nervousness, restlessness, insomnia, fatigue, feelings of weakness, tremors, weight gain, and decreased libido. You should also note that there have been some reported cases of increased suicidal thoughts and suicidal behavior from the use of SSRIs. If you find yourself contemplating suicide or acting out on suicidal thoughts after taking this kind of drug, contact your mental health professional immediately.

Tricyclic antidepressants. Like SSRIs, tricyclic antidepressants help maintain critical levels of neurotransmitters—this time both serotonin and norepinephrine—to boost mood and foster a feeling of calm. Unlike SSRIs, tricyclic antidepressants are not commonly prescribed due to their side effects, although they are still found to be effective for a limited number of anxiety conditions. They are often prescribed when newer forms of medications don't work. Tricyclic antidepressants take between three and twelve weeks to take effect, and popular brands include Anafranil, Norpramin, Tofranil, Pamelor, Vivactil, and Surmontil.

Known side effects of tricyclic antidepressants include drowsiness, dry mouth, disorientation or confusion, sexual problems, increased heart rate, increased appetite, fatigue, and seizures.

Monoamine oxidase inhibitors (MAOIs). The oldest type of antidepressants, MAOIs work by making sure there are high enough levels of serotonin, dopamine, and norepinephrine—which are all monoamines—in the body. Popular brands of MAOIs include Marplan, Nardil, Parnate, and Manerix.

Because MAOIs don't interact well with some foods, taking them means you will have to make some dietary restrictions. Specifically, by blocking the activity of the enzyme monoamine oxidase, the drug increases the levels of tyramine in the body, which in turn spikes blood pressure. Eating foods such as cheese, avocados, beer, soy, and tomatoes—all of which contain tyramine—can take one's blood pressure to dangerous levels.

Beta-Blockers

Beta-blockers are hypertension medications that are sometimes also used to manage anxiety. Beta-blockers can help reduce the muscular manifestations of anxiety, although they may not lessen feelings of dread and apprehension. They may be given as a single dose before an anxiety-provoking event—such as a test-taking situation—to relieve physical symptoms. Beta-blockers are popular for use in cases of phobia and performance anxiety. They are also commonly used to prevent post-traumatic stress disorder (PTSD).

Side effects of beta-blockers include asthma, irregular heartbeat, insomnia, sexual dysfunction, hypotension, abnormal vision, and hallucinations.

Up to this point, just about everything that has been suggested in terms of managing or overcoming anxiety has had something to do with dealing with and preventing the symptoms of anxiety within yourself. Sometimes, however, the triggers for anxiety are found in other people or situations. The last step toward overcoming anxiety is learning how to cope when other people trigger your anxiety.

Learn to Deal with Anxiety-Inducing People and Situations

Anxiety has a relational component to it—that is, anxiety can be triggered and aggravated by the presence of other people. This last step toward overcoming anxiety has to do with communication skills that can help you deal with the people who directly or indirectly trigger anxiety in you.

DEALING WITH NEW PEOPLE

Having to meet and talk to new people can be an intimidating experience. If you have social anxiety disorder, that's even more likely to be the case. You might feel that you're going to be judged by the people you talk to or that you're not going to pass their standards. The result: you feel awkward in the presence of new people.

The first thing you have to remember is that everyone has something to offer in a social situation. Each person is unique, which means everyone ultimately has something to contribute. Odds are, there is something you have done or can speak about that others will find interesting. You don't have to work too hard to impress people—you can often impress people just by being yourself.

Learn the art of a graceful introduction. Tell other people your name and a little something about yourself to get the ball rolling. You can, for example, share about your place of work or your favorite pastime. And if you can't find anything more to share, try instead to show your interest in other people. Ask questions, and listen intently to what others have to say.

Last, learn the art of small talk. You can talk about general topics such as current events—you may even discuss the weather. Comment on the other person's clothing style or line of work. The longer you are in discussion with someone, the deeper your conversation can get.

And if they aren't impressed? That's not a big deal either. Learning to let go of people's perceptions of you can go a long way toward helping you overcome anxiety in the long run.

DEALING WITH STEAMROLLERS

Dr. Robert M. Bramson, a psychologist and management consultant, wrote a popular book on the subject of personalities that you might meet, particularly in a business environment. *Coping with Difficult People* lists more than a dozen personality types, coining names for them and explaining how to deal with them.[24] One of the most prevalent types found in an office environment is the "steamroller" or "bulldozer." These are the people who aggressively demand that things go their own way and are not afraid of how many people they attack, just as long as they get what they want. If you feel like your boundaries are not being respected, then chances are you are dealing with a steamroller.

The main communication skill that you have to learn when dealing with steamrollers is assertive communication. You have to clearly and firmly communicate what you are willing and not willing to do. You have to say no when you mean no, and yes when you mean yes. You must also be able to communicate responsibly whatever it is that you are feeling at a given moment. Being in touch with your feelings and knowing what your boundaries are ahead of time can make dealing with contentious people all the less anxiety-inducing.

DEALING WITH OTHER ANXIOUS PEOPLE

As mentioned earlier, anxiety can be contagious, and if you're in the company of other anxious people, there is a good chance you will end up feeling anxious yourself. If you see your teammate panicking, for example, it can be hard to focus on your work. If your family members are overly worried about a situation, chances are you will get overly worried yourself.

One of the best ways you can deal with fellow anxious people is to learn some de-escalating techniques. Speak in a calm, even voice to communicate that the situation is still under control. Offer a listening ear to their worries and apprehensions. Be able to share the simple ways to get instant calm, which were discussed in the previous section. Instead of drowning in other people's anxiety, you can assist them in getting through their own episodes. In fact, doing so is a great way for you to step outside of your own anxiety and get some control over your own symptoms.

Of course, everyone is different, and there may be a type of person not listed here who causes an anxious reaction in yourself. That's okay. The most important thing to remember when overcoming anxiety caused by people and other situations is to communicate calmly and clearly, and know that this will pass.

Conclusion

Anxiety is difficult to experience, and sometimes even more difficult to cope with. It can take over all aspects of your everyday life, from work and school to relationships and home life. It can literally cost you, due to the inability to concentrate and produce the output that is needed from you. It can lower your self-esteem and make you think that you have no value in this world.

The good news is that anxiety is a treatable condition. As shown in the previous seven steps, you have many options for managing and ultimately overcoming anxiety—thought-management techniques, feeling-focused techniques, and prescription medication. Help is also accessible through counselors, counseling-trained religious leaders, psychiatrists, and other mental health professionals.

This book talked about the importance of understanding the nature of anxiety, from its types and symptoms to its root causes and various triggers. It went on to discuss many simple but effective ways of managing anxiety—from creating an instant calm to getting in touch with your thoughts and feelings to trying out calming mental strategies. Of course, simply managing the symptoms usually isn't enough. To really overcome anxiety, substantive and sustained lifestyle changes often need to occur: reevaluating the food you eat, exercising more often, and rethinking the ways that you communicate in situations that can trigger anxiety.

An anxiety-free life is attainable, and this book has given you the tools to begin living the life you deserve. With a little patience, an awareness of yourself and your surroundings, and a whole lot of follow-through, you can be well on your way to working through and overcoming the many different aspects of this debilitating condition.

Notes

1. Walter Bradford Cannon, *Bodily Changes in Pain, Hunger, Fear and Rage: An Account of Recent Researches into the Function of Emotional Excitement* (New York: D. Appleton and Company, 1915).

2. Ibid.

3. "The Numbers Count: Mental Disorders in America," National Institute of Mental Health, accessed September 4, 2013, http://www.nimh.nih.gov/health/publications/the-numbers-count-mental-disorders-in-america/index.shtml#Anxiety.

4. "Anxiety Disorders," National Institute of Mental Health, accessed September 4, 2013, http://www.nimh.nih.gov/health/topics/anxiety-disorders/index.shtml.

5. Ibid.

6. Ibid.

7. Ibid.

8. "Depression," National Institute of Mental Health, accessed September 4, 2013, http://www.nimh.nih.gov/health/publications/depression/index.shtml.

9. "Anxiety Disorders."

10. Joe Richman, "'Identical Strangers' Explore Nature vs. Nurture," Radio Diaries, NPR, October 25, 2007, http://www.npr.org/2007/10/25/15629096/identical-strangers-explore-nature-vs-nurture.

11. "Mitral Valve Prolapse: Risk Factors," accessed September 4, 2013, http://www.mayoclinic.com/health/mitral-valve-prolapse/DS00504/DSECTION=risk-factors.

12. "Depression."

13. "Mother Teresa of Calcutta Quotes," ThinkExist.com, accessed September 4, 2013, http://thinkexist.com/quotes/mother_teresa_of_calcutta/.

14. Norman Cousins, *Anatomy of an Illness: As Perceived by the Patient* (1979; repr., New York: W. W. Norton and Company, 2005).

15. Robert Dilts, John Grinder, Richard Bandler, and Judith DeLozier, *Neuro-Linguistic Programming, Volume I: The Study of the Structure of Subjective Experience* (Capitola, CA: Meta Publications, 1980).

16. Leo Buscaglia, interview by Phil Donahue, *The Phil Donahue Show*, August 16, 1990.

17. Stanley Rachman, "The Evolution of Cognitive Behaviour Therapy," in *Science and Practice of Cognitive Behaviour Therapy*, eds. David M. Clark and Christopher G. Fairburn, (New York: Oxford University Press, 1997), 1–26.

18. Robert Heinlein, *The Notebooks of Lazarus Long* (Wake Forest, NC: Baen, 2004, collected from *Time Enough for Love* (1973; reissue, New York: Ace Books, 1987).

19. R. D. Laing, *The Divided Self: An Existential Study in Sanity and Madness* (London: Tavistock Publications, 1959; repr., New York: Penguin, 1965). Citations refer to Penguin edition.

20. "Caffeine Content of Drinks." EnergyFiend, accessed September 4, 2013, http://www.energyfiend.com/the-caffeine-database.

21. "Sodium in Diet," MedlinePlus, last modified June 23, 2012, accessed September 4, 2013, http://www.nlm.nih.gov/medlineplus/ency/article/002415.htm.

22. Morgan Kelly, "Exercise Reorganizes the Brain to Be More Resilient to Stress," Princeton University: Current Stories, July 3, 2013, http://www.princeton.edu/main/news/archive/S37/28/70Q72/index.xml?section=topstories.

23. "Working Wellness into the Workday," *Body and Mind,* March 11, 2012, http://www.pennlive.com/bodyandmind/index.ssf/2012/03/working_wellness_into_the_work.html.

24. Robert M. Bramson, *Coping With Difficult People: The Proven-Effective Battle Plan that Has Helped Millions Deal with the Troublemakers in Their Lives at Home and at Work* (New York: Dell, 1981).

CPSIA information can be obtained
at www.ICGtesting.com
Printed in the USA
BVHW04s1533240818
525530BV00004B/25/P